Searching for Light

Michael's Information
for a Time of Change

Carol Heideman

TWELVE
STAR
PUBLISHING

ISBN 0-9643455-0-1

First Printing 1994
Second Printing 1995

Cover Art and Design by Julie Irwin Scott
Layout by Adeline R. Bailey
Edited by Nancy W. McCarthy

Interior Art: Rose Cross Cipher

Printed in the United States of America on recycled, acid-free paper.

Contents

Section Four: Onward and Upward

Preface

I always wanted to believe in magic. Over the past eight years, magic cascaded over me at every turn—amazing new abilities, extraordinary new people, trips to fascinating places, and most recently, publication of this book. How astonishing to realize these magical events follow a cosmic blueprint of my own design! You see, what I call magic is the way of our future, what everyone can experience. Magic happens when life flows easily, smoothly, and joyfully. We create magic for ourselves. This book is both born of magic and seeks to teach magical lessons. We are *all* magicians who forgot the magic.

I am a channel, working with a guide named Michael since 1987. The connection to Michael opened suddenly but gently in the spring of that year. Prior to that time, very little about me pointed in this direction. I was a shy, bookish child prone to reading fairy tales and fantasy. My family atmosphere promoted open communication, honesty, and thinking for yourself. Our family seemed more eccentric than others, but only because we had no secrets. With age, I grow increasingly grateful to my mother for such wonderful childhood lessons.

I married, raised two stepchildren, and divorced. Those nine years were filled with practical lessons in dealing with people, public speaking, teaching, parenting, and business. All those pieces fit together nicely in my current situation: I am self-employed as an interior decorator. I have three teenaged stepchildren in my current marriage. I occasionally conduct metaphysical gatherings and do other types of public speaking. Gentle lessons have prepared me for today.

I had enjoyed being single for over five years when the magic started in March 1987. I met my husband Mike, and we married only four months later. We were introduced by a mutual friend, who later told us of her intense compulsion to find someone for Mike. Eternal gratitude from Mike and myself to our friend Marlene, for everything in our plans depended on her to come through with that introduction. It was truly love at first sight! We actually *waited* until July 7, 1987, just to have a magical wedding date.

Different from me, Mike had been reading metaphysical books for several years—the Seth material, Ram Dass, and Michael books by Chelsea Quinn-Yarbro. Six to nine months after I'd read the first two Michael books by Quinn-Yarbro, Mike and I both learned to channel. In general, Mike channels art and creativity-related topics. I gravitate toward personal growth topics. Individually, we have developed various channeling techniques, using whatever fits our need at any given moment, from pendulums to voice channeling. I used automatic-typing to channel the information in this book.

In 1988, Mike and I held our first Michael gathering. There were seven people, including us. To this day, I'm amazed at how some of those people found us. Convoluted pathways of coincidence and accident . . . magic at work, I suppose! The Michael gatherings have been continuous since that first one, always drawing an interesting collection of people who ask intriguing questions. My thanks to everyone involved, because good questions are invaluable to a channel.

Magic seemed to put the right person in touch with me at the right time. People would arrive for very precise information at a particular point in their lives. I imagine myself at a little kiosk halfway up a mountain, handing out maps, specific to certain places along the spiritual pathway. I enjoy thinking of this book as a cosmic atlas which helps its readers get to their destination, wherever that may be.

In 1990, Mike and I travelled to Norway, sponsored by a metaphysical group in Oslo. Our exciting adventure completed some karma, broadened our teaching experience, and crystallized some lifelong friendships. We returned to Norway in 1992, stretching ourselves again with a two-day seminar on "How to Channel." Every part of each trip to Norway is pure magic: how the Norway connection started, all the wonderful people we met there, our comfort with the country and its people.

In December 1992, I created the first of 24 monthly newsletters. These are not transcripts of spoken sessions, but channeled writings intended to be read and studied. Michael "suggested" the newsletter, and it was over a year before I realized a book had been under construction all the while. This book was written in bite-size pieces with a deadline each month. Once again, my magic took a slower, more gentle route–efficient, too. In the spring of 1994, I became intrigued with computer modem communication. Through metaphysical bulletin boards and electronic mail, I met wonderful people from all over the country. Magic works through computers, too. My publisher literally knocked at my door through electronic mail.

And so, we arrive at today–this book and its message. I believe that the energy of the channel always influences the channeled material, so I wanted each reader to know a little about me. I hope to assist you who wish for happier lives. I've tried to provide clear and practical information–ideas that can make a difference NOW. I offer ways to increase JOY on our planet. Most of all, I wish for you to have magic in your life; to remember that you are a magician who knows how to create joyful magic for yourself. I hope my book helps you do exactly that.

Carol Heideman
Dallas, 1994

To Mike, my partner in everything.

Section One

Planetary Transformation

Chapter One
Earth's Transformation
Is Underway!

We are an entity, a collective of more than 1000 individual souls. We use the name Michael for your ease, as names are not really used where we exist. We currently work with many of you there within the physical plane; we have lived on Earth, and some of us shared past lives with many of you. We complete an agreement by providing this information to you. We are not here to tell you what to do or what to choose; we come to deliver information. This information will awaken some who have overslept. For others, the information will provide a map to any destination you choose. For all, it is a gift given in love.

Your planet is undergoing massive changes, structural energy changes which alter the very nature of reality on Earth. These changes are not coming—*they are already here!* It is our intention to assist you in maneuvering through this transformation. We bring information with both planetary and personal perspectives; we want you to see the expansive panorama of the planet as a whole, as well as a more intimate view of your own back yard. Our foremost desire is to provide practical and useful information for improving your spiritual growth. We bring a beacon of light to help you complete your lifeplan, which is the work you came to do HERE on this little planet on the fringes of the Milky Way, and NOW at this time of change.

We begin with this question: What is happening to your planet? You may have heard some explanations of the current phenomenon there on Earth at this time—tales of the Fifth Dimension or shifting magnetic poles. Some groups speak of this transformation as the biblical Rapture or Armageddon. These are all different "fairy tales," each referring to the same underlying concept from differing perspectives. Our simplest explanation is this: Earth is growing up, and this is the tricky time called adolescence.

Understand that our description must be a metaphor, explaining only the basic concepts of a Truth much larger than you can comprehend while on the physical plane. You see, while you exist inside the time/space continuum, you are restricted by certain boundaries. These boundaries provide the necessary focus for experiencing physical existence, but they also work much like blinders that block you from fully understanding universal events and concepts. For this reason, we repeat: Our explanation is a metaphor, and not to be taken in a literal manner.

From a cosmic viewpoint, Earth is a rather remote planet on the outskirts of the Universe. From that same cosmic perspective, Earth is not a particularly advanced planet in spiritual evolution. However, the planetary transformation makes Earth the focus of attention for conscious entities everywhere in the Universe! Although the planet is moving through a normal process of evolution, it occurs at the same time as an interplanetary configuration of energy—an event that occurs only once in several millions of years! This energy conflux is currently focused on Earth, allowing your planet to support a wonderful experiment in spiritual growth.

Thus, a normal growth phase for your planet has been strongly intensified by something rather like an eclipse between millions of planets simultaneously. This focuses universal energy onto one spot much like a prism operating in reverse; currently, the point of focus is your planet! Added to this are non-physical components that increase the energy level even more. It is an exciting time to be living on planet Earth; you worked very hard and planned for thousands of years to be here for these events!

Just like you, millions of other beings wanted to be here for the fun, so the planet is bulging with souls at this time. In fact, there is a huge team of lightworkers who came to conduct an experiment during this energy shift. The transition of Earth is the biggest event of the millennia, and you may be surprised to learn that you are not just seated near the stage—*you are on the stage!* Your performance involves how you handle today's lessons and choices—with the entire Universe watching intently. You are here on Earth NOW because of strong desire to be involved in this experiment and performance. How do you know if you are part of this group of lightworkers? If you are reading this book, you are almost certainly a lightworker. Anyone who is interested may join in the experiment. Desire to join is the only requirement for membership in this group. If you want to belong, you do.

This is the experiment: *To create an entirely new path for growth with joy complete with new methods of spiritual evolution.*

Growth: with Joy or Pain

The physical plane has various layers or levels. The more dense levels of energy focus on *growth with pain*; levels of less density use more refined energies, and the focus is on *growth with joy*. Souls must learn how to use joy in order to move to higher planes. Lightworkers seek to bring growth with joy into a level of physical reality which has seldom experienced it. You seek to make joy the normal mode of growth for Earth. You timed the experiment to coincide with the planetary growth surge, using the momentum of that energy to propel the plan. Millions like yourself have agreed to shift personal growth into joy mode at this time.

The timetable of your plan predicted a period of about five years for the planet to move *into* its adolescence, beginning about mid-1989. In the middle to late-'80's, many lightworkers awakened.

The first active phase of the plan kicked in; the gathering of lightworkers began. Before that time, lightworkers engaged in personal preparation, often in isolation. The planet has completed this five-year period of transformation! As you read this, you are already deep into the new intensified planetary energies, into the depths of planetary puberty! The full process will take many years to complete; our best estimate is from 25 to 50 years. Our job is to provide the larger perspective. We are your alarm clock, awakening you to your true purpose to be living on this particular planet, at this particular time. You stand at the threshold of a new reality.

On this planet, you create your reality in a more obvious manner than ever before. Here is a metaphor to explain this: Your planet existed for millions of years in a part of the Universe where the energy speed was 10 mph. During the transformation, your planet is moving into a faster part of the Universe. Acceleration began about five years ago, and reached 90 mph in around April of 1994 where it leveled off. The planetary energy is now turbulent and somewhat erratic, but over time this will smooth out. The acceleration phase is very tricky and constant readjustments are necessary. Each of you moves through your personal adjustment process on an individual basis. The planet's overall speed is a reflection of the average speed for all persons living. The standard speed is 90 mph for now; using growth with joy, lightworkers seek to achieve 100 mph! That is your grand experiment! The time for the push to 100 mph begins NOW.

Dharma and Karma

As a corollary to our previous explanations, we offer two additional concepts: *Dharma* and *Karma*. Our definitions of these terms may be a bit different than you have heard previously.

Karma is the energy you send out to others, including the cosmic consequences of your energy. For most humans, karmic energy goes out as emotions and actions directed at other people.

A complex aspect of karma is self-karma, which is core energy going out to some fragmented aspect of yourself such as one lifetime or one action taken. Self-karma creates an internal energy block, while karma created with another person creates an external energy barrier much like a closed door. When karma exists between two persons, there is an energy bond or "karmic ribbon" that needs to be "untied" or removed. This opens the closed door. Most karma between souls comes from actions that take away free choice. Any action can be taken without karmic consequences if done by agreement. For example, sometimes murder creates karma by taking away another person's choice to live; in another situation, there may be an agreement in place for one person to murder another, which would then be karma-free. Philanthropic karma—the highest form of karma—comes from truly loving acts done through choice, not done to untie karmic ribbons or for manipulation.

Dharma, if you are unfamiliar with the term, is commonly used by various Eastern philosophies and religions, with subtle variations in meaning from group to group. Our perspective focuses on the energy *underlying* these different interpretations. Dharma is the energy you *save* by following cosmic principles, creating a feeling of Oneness with the Universe. The only value judgement within the Universe is *efficiency*—not good/evil, not Heaven/Hell. Dharma requires the most efficient use of energy in any form. Dharma is gained when you achieve a desired outcome without using extra energy to overcome inner blocks and energy barriers. Creating dharma is the most joyful thing you can achieve in the Universe. You must follow the inherent nature of the Universe, including your own nature. You need to completely accept and unconditionally love yourself, as a prerequisite for feeling unconditional love toward everything else in the Universe. Dharma occurs when you find your position in the cosmic orchestra, discovering that your personal instrument and your favorite song are the perfect complement to the rest of the Universe! You achieve dharma by following your bliss. Lightworkers intending to achieve 100 mph are seeking dharma. Our job is to assist you in achieving this goal.

Chapter Two

A Massive Group Plan

Lifeplans

Prior to each incarnation, you create a lifeplan, a blueprint for that particular lifetime. As your soul evolves, more and more effort goes into these blueprints. Over many lifetimes, your plans become increasingly intricate, yet they are flexible because the physical plane is an unpredictable place! How do you know what you've planned? Well, you've arranged for us to come along and remind you!

At this time, you are working to get used to 90 mph. At your request, this book arrives at the stage when you need information about the next step, at a time to help you adapt smoothly and easily to the new energies. We intend to promote positive thought with effective timing. We are "planting seeds" of positive energy in your mind with our information. In addition to the conspicuous meanings within the material, there are additional layers of coded messages in our information.

A particular phrase or word triggers a strong interest or reaction, indicating subconscious recognition of a coded message. This is how codes operate. For some of you, the message's purpose is to awaken you, to start you thinking about your lifeplan (like your alarm clock in the morning). For others, the coded phrase stimulates you to take action in a specific way (like the sound of the gun at the start of a race). Sometimes, a "secret word" helps you recognize the end of something (like the final bell at the end of the school year). Each type of signal is a way to synchronize the actions and lifeplans of your group of lightworkers, souls working to reach 100 mph. Remember that your desire to participate assures your place within this group.

How can you be sure to get the message if it's in code? Follow your intuition, for it can decipher the hidden meaning. Using your intuitive nature, rather than blocking it off, allows you to receive messages more easily. The superficial message is helpful, interesting information, used as sweets to attract you! The most important "secret codes" are wrapped in an outer layer of tremendous appeal to you, ensuring that you will partake of the buffet! These codes work without your conscious mind, bypassing barriers created by negative belief systems. Surprisingly, codes operate very smoothly without the involvement of your conscious mind, but conscious awareness helps you increase efficiency. As your intuitive skills improve, you will identify the codes more easily. Codes are an effective and efficient way to streamline and calibrate intricate plans. We explain them to you here because your group seeks to increase enjoyment of the process by looking at mechanisms that are often invisible, like taking the back off a watch to see the precise movement of the tiny gears. This is one way your group adds joy to your plan . . . simply by watching the plan take form!

All of you will be adjusting to the new speed for some time. Right now, use every technique you've learned in recent months and years to maintain your personal energy level. Your goal is to stabilize your life, particularly areas that trigger negative reactions. *For many of you, this is the best time possible to clean up any "junk" left over from your past!* The active phases of most lifeplans are beginning! You will *not* want to be stuck cleaning up old stuff once new stuff is happening. Dig into your issues—NOW!

Before each incarnation, a soul makes plans and agreements in order to accomplish specific learning experiences. Karmic interactions require intense planning to establish particular types of relationships and situations for completing the karma. Skillful lifeplanning is learned with practice over many incarnations. In a well-planned lifetime, you organize hundreds, even thousands, of separate components to come together for a particular result: parents, relatives, friends, personality traits, jobs, children, and more!

Lifeplans are based on your individual abilities and skills, competence developed during your current lifetime, and your past lives. With few exceptions, the plan is made before you are born. It is then played out without conscious knowledge of the plan itself. Consequently, adjustments to the lifeplan are not easy to make. Your group decided that each of you needed knowledge of the overall plan, as well as your own personal lifeplan. Coded messages can take you only so far however, so you must start figuring out your personal lifeplan. Some of you already have a clear idea of your work; others may need to know more. In Section Three of this book, we present techniques for learning more about your lifeplan.

Your lifeplan is like a blueprint for building a house. Even with a complete and specific plan, very few houses end up being identical to the blueprint. As construction progresses, changes and adjustments become necessary. Some problems become apparent during construction, requiring creative solutions that minimize changes in other areas. When the house begins to take shape, you can walk through the partially completed structure and visualize other changes that make a *good* plan even *better*. Remember this example as you begin the active phase of your lifeplan. Flexibility is helpful as you adjust and fine-tune your plan.

Waves

What are the principal types of lifeplans? What are you looking for as you seek out the details of your own lifeplan? Most members of your group plan to work with the new, stronger planetary energy. For many of you, this is the basic premise of your lifeplan. There are orderly groups of people with related lifeplans which we call *Waves*, for they tend to flow one after another like ocean waves. We must speak in general terms in this section, for these are broad categories. Some people planned to work with energy as energy, but many will work with highly specific energies *within* particular categories: music, food, home furnishings, apparel, plants, art, retailing, advertising, computers, children, education, publishing, counseling, health, jewelry, cosmetics, business management, automobiles, service industries, travel, movies, recreation, and almost any other field you can name. Later, many of these fields will overlap or blend into new combinations. For instance, imagine art or jewelry that contain healing energies, creating an overlap into the health care field! Following is a detailed description of each wave, including how to recognize the members of each.

The *First Wave* is at work now, for everything begins with what these people create! They have waited a long time—not so patiently, either! This group consists of energy workers who create new techniques and methods for manipulating the intensified energy. Most of these people have worked with energy over many, many lifetimes. These souls have spent the last few years reviewing existing energy techniques, gathering knowledge about many different systems and methods. Members of this group may need to develop past-life recall through self-regression. (More about how to do this in the Energy Work section.) Recalling energy skills and techniques from past lives is very useful, providing a good foundation for improvisation and innovation. This group is at the forefront of the entire plan, figuring out exactly what the new energy can do; everything else comes out of what they can discover.

Most First Wavers are fairly easy to identify. These people are often so deeply involved in metaphysics that the so-called real world around them is almost meaningless! These people are often part of the counter-culture, preferring to live and work in a manner some would find unusual or eccentric. You see, *anything* they explore or play with is potentially a new energy creation! Members of the First Wave are often drawn to power spots on the planet, for planetary energy is their raw material. Many First Wavers are gathering at some highly energetic locations, some well known and some not. However, individual preferences vary greatly depending on the type of energy each likes to work with, so you will find these energy workers all over the planet. First Wavers are generally quite sensitive to their environment; many have felt a need to relocate since the new energy arrived. All directions are available to First Wavers! Some are experiencing a "lost" sensation, an emptiness, a lack of direction. Most members of Wave One have entered what we call "The Void," the state of emptiness which precedes creation.

The *Second Wave* is gathering, shaping themselves into teams. Their high-activity phase begins when Wave One offers them some findings or methods, so most are making final preparations by warming up their skills. Obviously, the timing for Waves Two and Three depends on how things go with the First Wave; this is why flexibility is a necessary part of lifeplans. The Wave Two group figures out how to disperse the findings of the First Wave. The Second Wave connects the relatively small First Wave to the large Third Wave. The goal of Second Wave is to create ways to communicate the new energy methods to a broad group of teachers. Second Wavers teach the teachers *what* and *how* to teach, inventing new instruction methods in the process. How can one prepare to teach something that does not yet exist? Second Wavers can work on obviously-needed skills: communication skills, relationship skills, leadership skills, and a strongly-developed intuitive nature. As in a relay race, timing is very critical—especially when the baton is about to be handed off. The Second Wave may be feeling "stuck" right now, impatiently waiting for the second leg of the race.

The work of some individuals in the Second Wave can be divided into two subgroups we'll call A and B. Wave Two-A focuses on receiving the data from the First Wave. Wave Two-B focuses on distribution to the Third Wave. Some people in Wave Two cover the whole range, from one end of the spectrum to the other. Since Wave Two is the buffer between two extremes, it requires the maximum degree of flexibility for adjustment of plans. In many ways, Wave Two is the trickiest, the most difficult to organize. It is the transformation point, changing the new innovations into something palatable for the masses fearful of change. A special sort of alchemy and creativity is required by Wave Two members.

Second Wavers have some very specific traits. They invariably have some background in teaching. We do *not* mean that all Second Wavers are school teachers however. Look a bit deeper for instance, at the underpinnings of many jobs and professions to see if they involve teaching. Does the work involve passing information, perhaps reorganizing it along the way to make it more "edible" to those who receive it? Does the job involve answering a lot of questions or describing things? Many Second Wavers have varied employment histories, often jumping from one field to another, but there is usually something buried beneath the surface that is common to all. Our broad definition of teaching is often found to be that common thread linking one job to another. In addition, this group is always searching for the latest, the newest, the most innovative of any given thing. This tendency can be a general attitude or it can be specific in focus, holding to a particular topic or area of interest. Either way, this affinity for newness works to keep the Second Waver on the lookout for the fresh inventions of the First Wave. In general, members of the Second Wave tend to have friends and contacts within both other waves. Second Wavers are often comfortable with people at both ends of the spectrum, ranging from the more "out there" metaphysical interests of the First Wavers to the very mainstream behaviors that dominate the Third Wave. People in Wave Two literally have one foot in each world, and can float easily from one to another.

The *Third Wave* is just beginning to gather. They will come together over the next three to five years. Everyone in this group is interested to see how things go with the first two legs of the relay race. Again, timing is critical! The waiting that is necessary for this group means more advanced notice for them, more time to get ready. What does Wave Three do? The Third Wavers are at the front line, dispersing the results of the work of the First Wave. Like Wave Two, this group teaches, but again, not necessarily in the traditional sense. Many Third Wavers plan to have businesses, selling products and services to the community at large; Third Wavers will often be dealing with "civilians" (people who are not consciously aware of the energy shift). Their work will not look or feel overtly metaphysical, but the positive effects will be obvious. Third Wavers may be relieved to realize that they can blend their spiritual interests with their more practical "real world" skills. This group may be experiencing the anticipation of change, but with less urgency than the other waves. Preparation at this point is similar to Second Wave activity, strengthening all related skills and getting connected to personal guides.

Third Wavers tend to have an intensely grounded view of metaphysics. These people are very, very "regular." In fact, Wave Three members often back away from groups or methods that are "too weird" for them. Most will have as many friends outside the metaphysical realm as they do inside. Third Wavers feel an intense need to stay connected to "normalcy," and friends with more traditional viewpoints provide them with a good sense of what regular folks will and will not accept. It is common for Third Wavers to feel some inner conflict between the "real world" and their interest in metaphysics. Sometimes, this ambivalence grows into a split in the fabric of the Third Waver's life, but that rift is seamlessly joined when the lifeplan kicks into gear. Remember, you have created lifeplans that fit perfectly with who you are today. Every Wave Three member will be involved in work that is appropriately mainstream, but with an inner layer of metaphysics at work.

How Does It All Fit Together?

Here is an example: Wave One creates a method of putting healing energy into objects made of wood. The technique can be used on any type of wood, and the shape of the final product does not matter, but the person who works with wood must have the ability to let the wood itself "tell" what energy it can best provide. Wave Two-A concocts an apprenticeship method to teach woodcrafters the technique. Wave Two-B does the actual instruction of how to use the method. The people who learn the method may be a combination of Wave Two-B/Wave Three (who use it *and* teach it to others) or simply Wave Three (perhaps as managers who set up factories that implement the method without teaching it directly to the workers). Finally, another layer of Wave Three retail people consciously choose products with full awareness of the energy of the product. Consumers respond intensely to these products without necessarily knowing why, and they benefit from the energy infused into a picture frame, table, or wooden bowl.

Maybe you already sense which wave feels like your group. If you are still curious, use the Guided Imagery technique explained later in this book to research your complete lifeplan. One limitation may be your ability to believe! If you cannot imagine yourself doing something, you will not see that part of the plan. Our recommendation is that you dream *bigger* and then you will be shown more of your entire lifeplan. We are aware of each lifeplan in your group, and all of you have very grand, substantial work ahead of you. If you have placed yourself within a small, self-limiting box of beliefs, you must take off the lid NOW! Your planet has started a period of transformation. Your belief systems will be challenged to keep up with the massive adjustments in every area of life—personal relationships, work, political systems, financial systems . . . everything! No matter who you are, each of you *must* expand your thinking to include what may seem impossible today. Over time, you will remember the full power of creative thought!

The White House

This term is a symbol, a metaphor that magnetizes and represents lightworkers currently on the planet. Everyone reading this book is most likely part of the White House, a very large group of souls who have carefully planned for this time in the planet's growth. The initial group has long been seeking out additional souls to "join the club." The plan is inclusion rather than exclusion; the goal is to let *everybody* play! There are over a million souls on the planet today who consider themselves part of this group. Our explanation of this metaphor will awaken some of you; others of you may now understand why certain images or visions appear in your meditations or your dreams. It is important to understand the complete history of your group in order to more fully appreciate the intricacy of your plans. One way to gather more joy from the energy shift is to observe the plans as they take shape. Advanced knowledge allows you to know what to watch for. Now you can enjoy seeing the outcome as it emerges.

The roots of your current plans lie at the beginning of all your incarnations on this planet, extending back to pre-history. A core group of lightworkers incarnated in a systematic way through thousands of centuries, with this time and place as the goal. Your group sought (and mostly accomplished) a particular level of spiritual growth in order to be in prime condition for your current experiment, the plan to elevate the spiritual level of the entire planet. Remember, you complete this plan only through synchronized individual action, achieving intense personal joy at the same time as multitudes of others do the same. This synchronized action creates a surge of joy energy that pulls the planet's energy into a higher focus than would normally be available at this level. Earlier, we called this "going to 100 mph."

At all critical times in Earth's evolving pathway, your group was highly active. At each soul level, you sought to create new methods and techniques, ways to propel yourselves forward with more energy-efficiency than other souls at that level. Understand that speed is not really a valuable asset, particularly outside the time/space continuum. You are not seeking *faster* spiritual growth; you are seeking to create *easier* methods of spiritual growth. This is closely related to the definition of dharma that we provided in the first chapter. Remember that dharma is the energy saved by following cosmic principles, and uses the inherent nature of the Universe and yourself to promote efficient growth. During other intense energy periods for your planet (such as ancient Egyptian times, the years during and around the life of Jesus, and others), your group has been practicing constantly at creating dharma.

One particular episode during Earth's life cycle, however, brought about a significant dharmic interlude. Your group had more success creating dharma during the peak years of Atlantis than during any other time period. The White House began there in Atlantis as an actual structure. The creation was a free-standing energy chamber that magnified internal thought patterns (similar to what a loudspeaker system does for voice patterns). The original White House was a crystalline structure about 25 feet square, similar in appearance to ancient Greek architecture. Columns of precision-charged crystals surrounded a central pedestal, which was formed by a single massive crystal. A person would enter the chamber, recline on the pedestal while carefully focusing all thought onto positive intentions and creations. For those with enough skill to focus their mind on only the positive, tremendous healing and manifesting would occur. However, even the slightest fear or negative thought would also magnify quickly, often causing severe problems, even death!

In managing the White House, your group discovered that you could not determine who should enter the chamber. At times, you actually forced people to enter the structure against their intuitive fearfulness of it, always with dire consequences. Please realize, you were almost all Young souls at this time. Young souls are busy gaining karma by testing their energy limits, so pushing others around in this manner was appropriate behavior for souls of your level. What you did next as a group, however, was an intense leap forward in spiritual growth . . . creating dharma! As a group, you determined that the White House should be left completely alone and open to all who would enter. You determined that any individuals passing by the structure would notice it only if drawn magnetically to its energy. They would then enter by personal choice. Even the subtle pressure of "advertising" the effects tended to draw forth those whom it would harm rather than help. Against the heavy control patterns of your age and society, you allowed your creation to operate unattended, with only natural cosmic forces at work.

Your group intensified the effect by building many more structures, leaving them to do their work without people there to control or monitor the chambers. Again, this went against the prevailing social and political mindset, which was based on following rules and heavy social controls. Over time, more than 5,000 individual chambers were constructed and programmed. As the healing chambers quietly did their work each day, positive energy on the planet multiplied tremendously. Results were dramatic, with individual souls jumping up three to five soul levels in one lifetime! This was an unprecedented spiritual leap for a group at your level! Shock waves were felt throughout the Universe, as the normal flow of energy was pleasantly disrupted by the "explosion" of high-grade dharmic energy moving out from Earth in all directions.

From the very beginning, your primary plans were for NOW, during the current influx of intensified planetary energies. Today's activities were planned as the main course to follow that Atlantean appetizer. Because your group succeeded in accessing such a tremendous quantity of dharmic energy in one burst, today's goals are entirely achievable. This is the shining moment—a result of your early stages of effort.

Your group concluded the Atlantis period, going out with a bang. You ended up with one of the largest karmic debt-loads of all time! The final explosion and destruction of Atlantis took many, many lifetimes to clean up; however, your group has completed that work in time for this energy shift. Now all thoughts and memories can return to the big dharmic success of the White House, rather than the big karmic lesson that followed! You intend to repeat the dharma, but without the karma this time!

This historical view is only one meaning of the White House metaphor, which is also a code representing your plans for the near future. Even the use of the term for the U.S. presidential mansion in Washington, D.C. has a coded meaning, for the political structures of the United States were designed and put in place by members of your group. In the astral realms, it was considered a fun way to make "White House" a commonly used term! Your group intends to provide catalysts for a multitude of social, political and economic world changes. Ultimately, these changes will occur gently but quickly, by using dharma. The impact will be felt worldwide, over a span of about 40 years. Of course, you are taking advantage of many natural cosmic forces—astrological energies (the Age of Aquarius), social and political energies (current timing brings your Baby Boom Innovation Generation into power), and non-physical energies (the energy shift). In addition, your plans reach across the globe using computer technology to link the members of your group. A single White House will become a village, then a city, then a country . . . until the planet is filled with the same powerful dharma energy that emanated from your little chambers in Atlantis.

As the plans unfold, the single most important thing to remember at all times is this: *If an action is not good for everyone involved, another solution must be created.* No individual must suffer for the good of the group, or the dharmic goal is lessened in strength. Each person's lifeplan must be completely joyful for the overall scheme to maintain itself. Such concerns will inevitably slow the process in the beginning. Intricate and detailed plans are being adjusted and executed NOW. The final preparation phase is happening for everyone! We have been asked by your Higher Selves to remind you of this need for harmony as you jostle your way into your place in line. Remember to look around for someone else that might need a little encouragement or assistance in getting that last bit of inner work completed.

You can learn more about your particular part in the White House group by using this image as part of your meditations or work with channeling. It may show up in your dreams. Ask your guides to show you whatever will help you to move forward with the plan. In all these instances, the concept serves as a symbol to unite your group toward your common positive goal.

Next, we will provide more details of your plans. There are several predictable changes we can explain, things which occur as a natural part of the energy shift. You will see these happening as Wave One people work to develop new energy methods never before used at this level. Earth will be a most interesting place for the next 200 years. Enjoy yourselves! This is the time you have awaited for eons!

Chapter Three

Changes To Expect

To present a clear, precise description of current energies on your planet, we must explain some of the underpinnings of the physical plane. Our lessons now move into defining the structure of the Universe—a massive subject! Please understand that these teachings are intended to help you perceive your own position in the flow of Universal Energy. You can validate our information by looking at your own daily experiences, observing the changes in the people and events around you, and also those within yourself. Our explanation is offered not only to show you where you have come from, but your spiritual destination as well.

Energy is the primary force of the Universe. Energy creates everything that you perceive with your five physical senses; however, it creates much, much more than just physical objects. For those who are equipped to perceive them, thoughts and feelings are as observable as physical objects; they exist in a refined vibrational zone. Physical plane energies operate in approximately 25 zones which include anything that exists within the time/space continuum. Less than 3% of the total energy range of the Universe is discernible from the physical plane, however, even for those with highly developed energy senses.

Energy Zones

Each part of the Universe operates in a particular vibrational zone, and Earth is currently experiencing upward movement of its vibration from one to another. Since this movement does not occur as a jump, but with more of a "scrolling" motion, many people in the middle of the spectrum have not yet realized there has been movement at the upper and lower ends. Those at the lowest range are reacting strongly, for they must speed up or "fall off."

Long before any ensouled beings came here, your planet entered a zone we shall label Zone Two. This energy zone has been operative on Earth for all time that souls of your type have inhabited the planet, even when these souls were not in human form. (Dinosaurs were ensouled, which explains your strong fascination for them.) Zone One energies function at a chemical and cellular level, usually at the "birth" of a planet. Zone Two attracts souls at the beginning of their journey back to Oneness. Zone Three energy is a more refined energy, radically different from Zones One and Two. From your current location, it would be almost impossible for you to even *imagine* anything beyond Zone Four or Five, even in the wildest science fiction.

The "scrolling" movement has shifted your planet into a precarious position, straddling Zones Two and Three. Earth is headed into Zone Three, but a certain amount of planetary cleansing and balancing must occur before additional movement can come about. The adjustment period is expected to be about 100 years. As you might guess, this time period which seems long to you is relatively short when compared to trillions of years spent in Zone Two. In about 2080, another massive "scrolling" will take place, similar to the movement we defined earlier as "going from 10 to 90 mph." This time, however, the high end of the energy range will jump to 250!

We offer another metaphor to help you understand the different energy zones and your current movement from one to another. Imagine the ocean, with the dense, solid matter that forms the ocean floor as the lower boundary. The air above is another boundary. These three forms of matter provide a good way to study the shift from one zone to another. Zone One (the ocean floor) is extremely dense, generally precluding any life forms except at the point where it connects to the zone above. Zone Two (the ocean) has a tremendous range of density and life forms. Some creatures in the lower areas of the ocean have never even experienced sunlight, and the majority of ocean creatures have no awareness that the air above exists. Few ever move into the lighter density of the air zone, even for an instant. If a creature moves into the air environment before it's ready to function there, it will not survive. Creatures must evolve, developing new skills to make this transition. Those of you on Earth at this time are like the first sea creatures to explore life outside the ocean. Have patience with the changes, and please be gentle with yourselves!

In earlier information, we spoke of choosing between growth with pain versus growth with joy. It is necessary to choose joy to stay with the movement into Zone Three, because growth with pain occurs *only* within Zone Two. Those souls who do not shift into a joyful focus must move to another planet with Zone Two energy, in order to continue growth at their current level. Of course, the upcoming second massive energy shift will be much more fun, more joyful, because *everyone* riding that one will be using growth with joy. The current shift is more pivotal, however, so you who are on Earth at this time have selected the "early shift" rather than the "late shift" in order to seek more dharma (or energy efficiency). In an interesting side note, there are a few of you who are planning to stick around in your current bodies until 2080 for the next movement. If you think you are one of those souls, take good care of your body!

For additional clarity, here is more about the energy zones with which you are working at this time. Imagine a line graph where 0–10 is the range of Zone One; Zone Two goes from 10–100; Zone Three goes from 90–250. We now speak of the *range* of energy, rather than a single precise number, or 90 mph as in our earlier example. The range includes all the speeds of energy that accumulate and result in an average of 90 mph.

Zone Two (10–100). Look at history. Look at your "human instincts." Look at how pain and fear serve to motivate action (or non-action)–in religion, in politics, in families, in relationships. Zone Two operates on a basis of hard lessons learned through karmic interactions. There are three main sections in Zone Two: Physical Survival (10–30), Emotional Survival (30–70), and Compassionate Connection (70–100). The only area that overlaps into Zone Three is 90–100. Before now, 90–100 energies were only used by souls in their final few lifetimes, such as great spiritual masters and teachers. Christ operated between 100 and 125 in order to remain visible in a physical form. Pushing the planetary energy into the 90–100 range as an average is a significant change.

The current planet energy range is 75–150. People with *any* energy below 75 will not stay on the planet for more than ten years into the future. To people who bravely seek to move into the unknown energies over 90, we recommend gentle, easy explorations with a comfortable retreat back to the solid, secure 80–90 range. Returning to our ocean example, imagine you are dolphins leaping happily into the air but returning often to the upper zone of the ocean. As you practice leaping, developing comfort in the air zone, you will increasingly remember your inherent air-breathing mammal nature which will help you make the transition.

Zone Three (90–250). Now try to imagine a utopian world, a place where energy flows with great harmony. People interact with one other efficiently and effectively, and also develop a unity with the planet itself. Zone Three operates on the basis of lessons learned through *dharmic* interactions. There are five sections in Zone Three: Goal Harmony (90–120), Goal Unity (120–150), Pattern Harmony (150–190), Pattern Unity (190–220), Action Unity (220–250). Harmony lessons serve to synchronize, while Unity lessons lead to complete Oneness. Here is an example of each section within Zone Three in order to show the perspective of each:

Goal Harmony = Everyone decides to go to the western part of the US.

Goal Unity = Everyone decides to go to a particular city in California.

Pattern Harmony = Everyone decides to use various types of transportation—cars, airplanes, trains, bicycles, etc.

Pattern Unity = Everyone decides to use speedy jet airplanes, often together in large groups.

Action Unity = Everyone teleports together to the goal, synchronizing goal, pattern and action.

Note that the "everyone" in this example refers to the soul grouping within which you are currently working. As people work on lessons in Zone Three, the group sizes will range from as few as two to three souls up to several thousand. Zone Three is about harmonizing group interactions, with each individual already operating in positive, joyous energy. It is about expanding joy by sharing it.

What lies beyond Zone Three? After another few hundred trillion years, the next zone shift moves the planet into a zone of even less density. Again, returning to our ocean/air example, this will be like a movement through the various layers of the atmosphere, out . . . out . . . to the airless, emptiness of space! Air-breathing bodies must again evolve, gaining new natural abilities in order to survive in space. At this point, however, it is a great stretch for you to have awareness of Zone Four energies. (Imagine the fish at the bottom of the ocean, living in complete darkness in the most dense part of Zone Two. How can they know anything of Zone Three, much less Zone Four?) You are in the midst of a great exploration. Please use this information to help you enjoy the process.

Personal Changes

The information about the White House in the last chapter was layered with many coded phrases and concepts, so a great number of you probably felt strong intuitive reactions as you read it. Remember, codes often operate like alarm clocks, awakening you to your purpose for being on Earth at this particular time. Your "wake-up call" will trigger a subtle internal change that comes from your own Higher Self. These small shifts in behavior or attitude accumulate over time, ultimately leading to major life changes. Like following a great river back to its humble beginnings as a tiny stream, you will someday look back to this time to find the roots of your growth with JOY!

You will likely find yourself feeling increasingly dissatisfied with any part of your life that does not contribute significantly to your lifeplan. Discontent helps you to detect changes that need to be made—work, companions, lifestyle or location. Try not to fight these feelings, because resistance may slow your progress. By refusing to acknowledge an upcoming shift, you create an abrupt, disruptive movement, but if you can recognize and accept the need for change, events will flow more gently. By monitoring and embracing your lifeplan, your actions will readily blend and harmonize with your goals and those of others. Remember, one of your group goals is to create and use mutually joyful solutions and plans. If you discover conflict, back up and reconsider. Pushing against resistance is seldom helpful, so use your creativity to manifest a more joyful solution.

You may anticipate the following types of changes as you progress with your lifeplan, for many of you share common situations that will have related adjustments.

1. *Blending of Work and Other Interests.* Over much of your lifetime, you've probably made distinctions between work activities, and play or hobby activities. As an example, your involvement with metaphysics is a strong interest, but life seems to require that you maintain work activities to support yourself. As this incarnation progresses, you will find these separate pathways merging into a single focus. Along the joyous path, the line between work and play disappears! To prepare, ask yourself: Do I have permission (from myself or any internal voices) to earn my living from playful activity? If you discover blocks to this idea, deal with them now. It is possible that such blocks stem from ingrained beliefs learned from your parents or from society.

2. *Final Exams.* Have you been dealing with particular issues a great deal over recent years? It's time now to show what you've learned! Much like an exam at school, you have a chance to pass or fail, to move forward into the next level or to start the same workbook over again. Look at your most pressing problem. Is this something you've faced before, maybe from a new person or job this time, but with the same underlying issue? If so, make very deliberate choices while using everything you've learned in recent lessons. Most of all, try not to repeat old behavior patterns, for that is the surest way to start over.

3. *New Faces in Your Life.* You may be disturbed when contact dwindles between you and old friends who've been close to you for many years. Your old friend may be stuck in negative

thought patterns or fail to pass a final exam to enter the same zone as you are in. It also makes room for the new people who are about to enter your life. These new friends and task companions will help you complete your lifeplan. Occasionally, an old friend is part of your lifeplan, but most of you will experience at least one loss in this area. In some cases, a very close, positive-energy friendship may gently change into a less intense friendship when personal interests shift. Remember to *allow* these changes to happen; don't fight them. Space is needed for your new contacts and friends to come into your life. These "new" faces will be very old friends from many, many shared past lives. Over the next couple of years, there will be many happy reunions coming up for all of you as these connections happen. Enjoy the arrivals without dwelling on the departures.

Planetary Changes

Interesting shifts in planetary consciousness will occur in the short-term (within 5 years) and the long-term (10 years or more). Because of your group plans, there are wide variances in possible outcomes. Your group targeted specific areas that are sure to change; however, we cannot discern exactly how small or large these changes will be. In the following information, we provide cosmic projections, much like sales projections for a business. These predictions are based on complex computations and observations of other planets as they experienced similar growth periods. You and your group's plans are the unknown factor in the equation, however! Our best guess is that you will manage to go beyond our conservative estimates. Most of the predictions that follow describe what has happened on other planets during this phase, and we will add what is known of your group plans as well.

Sixth Sense Becomes Mainstream: Whenever a planet moves to 90 mph, the intensified energy awakens everyone's awareness of the intuitive sensory perceptions (what is commonly known as ESP).

This means that all people develop energy perceptions on a more conscious level than ever before. For some, this will infiltrate the other five senses, sometimes causing an occasional overlap in sensory perceptions. (This frequently occurs as an after-effect with individuals who experience a near-death experience. Such people may "hear" a painting, or "see" a song.) This change is already happening. Small incremental increases continue throughout the short-term, so the shift will not be abrupt. Over the long-term, it will completely transform the arts, education, retail and marketing fields (which are the primary focus areas for the White House group). Your group has tremendous plans here, using the growing awareness to create energized objects and places that will attract customers in droves, even while most people are still unaware of the magnetism on a conscious level. Education techniques (for both children and adults) will be revamped to make use of these changes in perception. Changes in the arts will occur in "clumps," that is, as the technology of energy hits each branch, the areas that are interrelated will be influenced; at some point, the blending and overlapping of the energy will cause various art forms to become a single entity—just ART. In one phase of your plans, your group is blending healing energy with these other energy forms. You plan to send healing energy to everyone through products, places, teaching and performances.

New Economic Structure: To us, an economic structure is the mechanism that *moves* energy in any form (money, food, products and services, even the military) from person to person, city to city, country to country. For most planets, old systems fall apart before the new structures are created. Great chaos is required to literally force souls to develop a system of balanced interactions. Ultimately, the higher energy zones require complete abundance such that all monetary systems become useless; everyone has everything they want, so money isn't needed. Difficulties always arise from situations where energy imbalances occur habitually in great volume; compare two people within the same large corporation— the CEO making millions of dollars in a year, while a typist barely makes enough on which to live. Such patterns are very hard to break without a forced change. Your group has an interim plan for a cooperative business structure that will serve to buffer the shift into life with abundance. Your plan should avert the need for massive economic chaos. In the cooperative business structure, large businesses are owned by the employees. In this way, people can learn about the interconnectedness of all economic matters, leading to more and more blending until there is a global economic structure operating in balance.

New Political Structure: Political power is another form of energy, one that is highly connected to economic energies. Political changes will be triggered by economic changes; economics are the walking legs, while politics are the swinging arms which automatically react in rhythm to changing strides of the legs. Understand that economics fuels politics, not the other way around. On other planets, new political structures blossom only after new economics are in place, sometimes a full generation later! On your planet, a significant difference occurred with the creation of the United States at a comparatively early phase in your development. Other planets usually shift to this form of government after the arrival of the intensified energy. One part of your plan was to give this structure to the predominantly Young souls in the U.S., allowing them to play with it for over 200 years. Many of the founding fathers of the U.S. were members of your White House team! Of course, these Young souls have managed to "tinker" with this toy, fighting over it and often mishandling it. Democracy has been stretched and strained over the years, at times barely holding its shape. As the economy changes, however, the worldwide political structure has a basic framework within which to operate. The political adjustment will not be as traumatic as the economic shift. One twist ahead: Political leadership will require *honor*—within the short-term!

Cultural Changes: One of the most invigorating ways to enjoy yourself right now is to observe the people and events of today, as the move to more positive planetary activities and energies takes place. Here we will acknowledge and review some of the signs and signals of positive planetary growth. This collection of odds and ends share one common feature: all are examples of enlightening energy that heals the imbalance of Earth's collective energy.

❖ People are looking for ways to heal their souls. Psychology and recovery books are in the most rapidly growing segment of book sales in the United States. How many bestselling books have as their focus some form of healing or personal growth? Seminars and talks on these subjects are well-attended nationwide. More people than ever before are seeking to be whole and happy.

❖ Cultural leaders are rising to lead the way. Popular television talk-show hostess Oprah Winfrey is personally leading a powerful campaign to heal America. Using education and information, she continues to promote healthy relationships and deepening spirituality to the general public. Observe how often Oprah uses the word "heal." She's doing her job as a lightworker very well!

❖ The past is being reexamined, serving as an aid to each person on the planet to make better choices today. Popular films are presenting the recent past with power and heart. Director Steven Spielberg's movie "Schindler's List" provided the true experiences of the Holocaust, but with a focus on the uplifting efforts of a real man, an imperfect man, who saved more than 1,100 Jews from the Nazis. The new paradigm makes the past look different.

❖ Messages and lessons are coming from all directions—books, movies, television, art, and music. Listen to song lyrics, observe the way communication and relationship skills are being taught by some movies and television programs, notice the trends of what is popular. Look for the deeper meaning and the subtle energy that causes a strong magnetism for a particular song or book or movie. Notice how the public responds.

We suggest that you attune yourself to such wonderful confirmation of how things are going for the planet. All the work of the lightworkers (such as yourselves) is having its effect. Remember that you are doing your share when you clean up your own life, lighting your own candle to dispel the dark. Slowly, candles are lighting up, one by one, steadily increasing the light and reducing the darkness. Keep to your own work, but also take some time to look around and enjoy the enlightenment of the planet!

Chapter Four

How Light and Love
Work Together

Bringing Light into the planet is your primary job as a lightworker. For this reason, you must maintain positive energy as much as you can. It doesn't really matter what you spend your time doing because all activity is simply a way to allow energy to flow between people. All relationships, all business dealings, all lifeplans—these create opportunities for you to "en-*light*-en" your planet. By allowing yourself to recall your primary purpose, you will see situations with a better perspective. A large group of souls broadcasting light together can look like a fabulous fireworks display! Equally as important, however, is a single person sending light into a dismal situation. It looks like a candle flickering in the dark, but it draws forth those who are seeking light!

What is this light energy? It is a very specific grade or type of energy which contains *information*. Light energy leads to comprehension, understanding, and awareness. Using light energy is the gentlest way to reduce and/or eliminate fear energy. As lightworkers, you are here to blend the love energy of Earth with your light energy. Fear and love cannot exist together, as they are the two polarities of a choice; your incarnations here on this planet provide countless opportunities to select one or the other, love or fear. Light energy illuminates your choice, and light energy is more harmonic with love than it is with fear. In other words, light energy feels comfortable and pleasant to those souls using love energy, while light energy creates discomfort in those who prefer fear energy.

Light energy *is not* the same as love energy! These two can be blended together easily, but each still has a distinct "flavor." Love energy is what makes this Earth "school" so intense, so visceral; it can be compared to steel—strong but very heavy in a large quantity. Light energy is less physical, more cerebral; comparable to aluminum—slightly less strong but very pliable. On a daily basis, you lightworkers blend light energy and love energy into a wonderful "alloy," allowing the qualities of each to improve the other. The outcome is a strong but light experience of the physical plane. Your goal is to create intense yet joyful earthly experiences, and for this to be commonplace after the current transformation is complete. As you might expect, things are "heating up" right now to allow the two melted metals to blend. Only after things "cool down," in about 100 years or so, will a complete assessment be possible regarding how well the blending process succeeded.

When you send light energy to a situation or individual, you are inviting the Universe to "explain things" to those involved, yourself included! The Universe's explanation is much like an encyclopedia, opened to the right page; anyone involved must make their own effort to study the material, sometimes stretching their minds to comprehend it. At times, you'll read the information, but comprehension will elude you. Be patient, another page will open, giving you additional information. Sometimes, you'll understand while those around you refuse to even look at the encyclopedia! Frustrating as this may be, you will usually waste time and energy trying to "make" them study. It just doesn't work that way! You'll use that same energy more efficiently by sending more light energy toward them. The Universe will find another way to reach them with the information they need. Sending light is a powerful action; it combines loving acceptance of the other person with an ardent effort of assistance.

Please recall that you are all *experienced* lightworkers. You have worked with light energy in other systems long before your series of lifetimes here in this part of the Universe. You see, Earth is the Love Planet; agape (unconditional love) is the primary lesson for all souls choosing this experience. You've learned your lessons about love through a series of incarnations on this planet, much like spending years learning the native language in a foreign country. Light energy is your native language! Using light is very natural and easy for you. Now is the time to begin "translations," much like sharing the stories of your home culture, but using the language of this planet to tell them. Naturally, some words of your "language of light" will enter the translation. You will create a blending of the two languages. That is how love and light energies are coming together now on Earth.

Homework: At this time, it's important to *seek recall of "home"—your society of lightworkers and what it feels like.* Please understand that it is not as "physical" as your earthly experiences. Your natural form as a lightworker is non-physical, as well as outside linear time. This is not an easy homework assignment, but even small flashes of remembrance in dreams or meditation will intensify your ability to move light energy.

How is Light Entering Earth?

There are many teachings being offered simultaneously at this time. You may find yourself receiving numerous layers of information that vary just enough to create confusion. We hope to alleviate some of this confusion by providing an overview of the current metaphysical and mainstream teachings, highlighting their techniques and illustrating their fine points. We want to improve your understanding of the transformation process since most of you intend to teach others, in one way or another, as part of your lifeplan. As older and more experienced souls, you carry a responsibility to help the younger souls of the planet. This section also

touches on why there is such tremendous variety in spiritual information about the current planetary changes.

Metaphysical Teachings

A great deal of information is available to you from high-level
guides, in many written and verbal forms. People at the forefront
of the your group plan are using such guidance as a primary source
of information. In fact, a goal for the White House group is to have
each participant personally connected to his/her own higher guidance. The primary teachings are as follows:

✧ *Energy Techniques and Methods.* These include One-Brain,
Reiki, Alpha-biotics, etc. Also included are breathing techniques, yoga, meditation, channeling (all methods), and manifesting. This is a very large category, and some people spend
years and years gathering a variety of techniques and methods from this huge "buffet." A broad range of teaching techniques are used, from the use of religion and dogma to very
business-like, scientific approaches. In general, this information comes from "outside" rather than "inside." This can be
a problem when students give over too much power to their
teachers or guides. As a result, it may take years of study to
influence the student's belief system and create permanent
behavior change. Massive changes are underway that will
significantly speed up the transformation process which con-
verts mental comprehension into behavioral and physical
changes. Wave One energy workers are now creating these
new methods. Innovations in energy manipulation and knowledge require new methods of instruction and new "school-
ing" businesses to arise.

✧ *Planetary Energy Information.* Teachings such as these focus on the planetary changes that are currently under way.

This information may include special terminology (e.g. transition, dimension, density, etc.), and often highlights upcoming Earth changes such as increased earthquake and volcanic activity. Such planetary data seldom changes how people act day to day, however. Belief system changes triggered out of fear rather than comprehension can create difficulties for the long-term. We expect to see somewhat less focus on negative with regard to Earth changes information, and an increase in positive information in this area which has been down-played up until now. A broader perspective brings forth this uplifting data, providing some global goals needed for the future-minded souls on the planet.

✧ *Interplanetary Information.* This category includes information about the political structures that connect many of the inhabited planets within the Universe. References to levels or divisions, sometimes with military terminology, are commonplace. Information in this category ranges from alien abductions (and other types of alien contact) to data about Earth's role within the interplanetary alliances. There may be details about different types of aliens (some good, some not so good), along with occasional conspiracy theories about our earthly governments and their relations with aliens. Information of this sort usually does nothing to assist the listener in his/her personal growth. It is frequently considered "safe" subject matter for those who are interested in metaphysics but who are unwilling to work on their own soul evolution. We expect to see an increase in individual contacts with aliens, but this will continue to be considered a "fringe element" for a while. Planet-wide contact with aliens is still some time away because your planet's overall consciousness is not yet ready for it. Too much, too soon would distract you from your most important work. As a whole, the answers you seek lie *within* individuals.

Mainstream Teachings

You may be surprised to realize that many people in non-metaphysical areas of study and work are also coordinated to the current planetary shift. All creative people receive flashes of insight about lifeplans and goals which are directed from their own higher selves. This means that "channeled" information comes through without conscious realization from the one who channels. Some never recognize their part in a larger pattern, while some eventually perceive the connectedness. There is great value in operating *within* the existing structures of society, for many barriers and walls fall away more easily. We suggest that you look for these types of teachings around you, for you will then be more likely to support them or at least, not fight them. We are not saying that these teachings (or new ideas) are necessarily aligned with your plans, but understanding them will increase your acceptance of them.

✧ *Organized Religions.* Noteworthy change is occurring within most organized religions. There is some form of recognition of the current planetary changes, usually found in the finer points of doctrine. Most Christian religions, for example, are talking more about "the Rapture," which is a very good metaphorical description of the energy changes. On some inner level, everyone is sensing the added intensity. There is a heightened feeling of expectancy toward the fulfillment of religious prophecies. Events like the sighting of the Madonna at Medjegorje are on the rise. Everyone is feeling a need to "clean up their act" and get more focused, which is a helpful approach to the energy changes. In a few cases, the added intensity takes the group deeper into their dogmatic beliefs, which leads them deeper into an imbalance that can seriously disrupt the organization, requiring adjustments and organizational healing. The disruptions provide valuable lessons and growth opportunities however, even amidst the chaos and problems. We foresee today's polarization of different religions softening into mutual respect and interaction as religious leaders seek to help solve worldwide problems.

❖ *Popular Entertainment.* Look closely at what's happening in the entertainment field. A tremendous amount of consciousness-changing is going on through books, movies, television, and music. This is one of the more exciting areas at work today, bringing about fantastic results in a gentle, harmonious way. Remember that the planet has never had such wondrously quick and strong communication available. There are many influential old souls "planted" in the arts and entertainment fields. The general focus is to educate people gently with entertainment. You can find "rap" music with uplifting spiritual messages (from highly visible groups like P.M. Dawn or Arrested Development), alongside the "New Age" music that is more obviously consciousness-changing. Some of the most popular television programs in the U.S. (*Roseanne* and *Home Improvement*) are laughingly teaching communication and relationship skills that are sorely needed by souls seeking joyful growth. In fact, many social problems that were invisible or considered unspeakable until recently are now considered major social issues by the mainstream, simply because of education through the media. An example of this is the awareness and concern about child abuse. As mentioned earlier, Oprah Winfrey is doing an important job in her education of the public. This area has proven highly successful over the last few years, and we foresee much, much more here in years to come.

❖ *Health and Medicine.* Significant changes are happening on this front. In fact, upcoming breakthroughs in the medical field are likely to do more to transform the joy level on this planet than anything else! Please understand that the field of traditional medicine is about to "discover" the connection between the mind and the body. When science gives its nod to the reality of this, people will be able to mentally create the degree of health they desire. One of the cosmic reasons for the tragedy of AIDS is that it directs the full force of traditional medical research into the auto-immune system—right where the connection of mind and body lies! Very soon, the regular medical field will figure out what many of you have known for years—that there is an energy field in and around a living body that can be measured and manipulated to improve health. In the same way that acupuncture and other Eastern medical techniques have slowly become mainstream during the last few years, you will see a speedy increase in other alternative health methods. Watch for the changes to come from doctors, those who are currently being "awakened" to begin their work in this area. The area of health and medicine will be almost unrecognizable within 20 years.

✧ *Schools and Education.* This is an area which currently lags behind the others in visible changes. You might think that computers and media aids have already made big changes in this area, but actually education hasn't even begun to transform. Notice how bored most young students feel after only a few years in school. Students do not routinely develop a love of learning, or an ability to teach themselves. This is a structural problem, an imbalance at the very root of the entire philosophy used today in deciding how to educate. In essence, core philosophical changes are needed. Additional pressures on the educational system develop as increasing numbers of adults need new skills in the rapidly-changing job market. Effective adult education has *never* been developed. The revolution begins very shortly. Education will take on more "soft" areas like creativity, self-esteem and life skills. The focus changes to "Teach a man to fish, and feed him for a lifetime." Wheels are already in motion that remain as yet unseen; this area will explode over the next three to five years.

❖ *Business and Government.* Huge reformations are just beginning in this category. For a few years, a hopeless sense of chaos and upheaval will blanket the planet. Please understand that many abrupt actions are creating pressure for needed changes in business and government. Some positive change comes out of avoidance of the *undesirable* rather than from a magnetic pull toward the *desirable.* As an example: Governmental policies and the current economy create a natural push toward self-employment. Large companies are no longer dependable for lifetime employment. People increasingly retreat from big business structures in favor of entrepreneurial businesses, gradually moving the country toward new ways of doing business where people interact with independence and flexibility. Over many years, large corporate structures will be replaced by a new business structure that does not yet exist. Ultimately, every working person will be an entrepreneur who freely participates in this new form of business, a sort of "consortium" that loosely connects people in an organized, yet flexible format. This new business structure will empower its members, but it will require good life skills and self-esteem, so this change must occur over the long-term. Obvious changes are happening at this time to international governments all over the planet. We foresee 25 to 35 years of political work and change, ultimately leading to a planetwide unification into a truly effective world government. The erasure of international boundaries will happen first in the business world. This is already happening! Once the planet becomes one large, interconnected business entity, political changes will happen quite naturally.

✧ *Family and Community.* A return to old-time values is being touted. We see this as a shift in soul consciousness. As more souls on the planet move from Young to Mature, there is a magnetic pull toward increased connectedness with the people around you. Over time, the definition of "family" will extend to close friends who are not blood relations. "Community" will grow to include more than just the few blocks around your home. Boundaries caused by skin color and economic status will be erased as educational changes have their effect. People will be interacting in business with more equality and choice. Most people will move in wider circles because of changes in both business and education. This area will not really *change* as much as it will *broaden* to be more inclusive. Inter-personal skills will improve all forms of social interaction. Parenting will improve. Divorce will decline. Close friendships will increase. Loneliness and suicide will decline. JOY will increase.

Chapter Five

Everybody Chooses Growth

Earth's new energy requires a minimum level of joy. Over the next ten years, people *must choose* to enter the positive energy state or leave the planet. Yes, we realize this is a strong statement. Yes, we knowingly reveal that the departure of many, many souls is highly probable. Yes, we understand how "negative" this idea sounds.

How Long Can Negative Survive?

Let's return to the fundamental decision you must make: growth with joy versus growth with pain. Notice that *both* options involve growth as different pathways to the same destination. Up to this point, the two paths overlapped, but the new planetary energy splits the shared pathway into two separate avenues. The route of growth with pain is a rough dirt road, full of holes and rocks that hurt your feet. The road of growth with joy is a freshly paved interstate highway, smooth and easy to drive at high speeds. Driving along at 90 to 100 mph is very different than walking or jogging along a dirt road! Some souls remain more comfortable with good 'ole dependable pain—guaranteed to move you forward, limited only by how much of it you can stand! If a soul prefers painful growth, *they are still moving forward.* Remember this if someone close to you clings to their painful ways.

You may ask, "Why do you say ten years? What happens then?" It is *not* what happens at a specific point ten years from now; it is what happens during those ten years. The two pathways (pain and joy) have already split apart, but currently travel in a parallel manner. At this stage, souls can still easily shift from one to the other. The two paths are moving further and further apart over time, however. Each passing day solidifies your position on one pathway or the other. Some souls are still jumping back and forth, but it gets harder and harder every week, every month, every year. Ten years from now, the critical point will come where it becomes virtually impossible to shift from one path to the other. If painful growth is the final choice, the soul must find another place to continue seeking lessons, to some part of the physical plane where the path is still growth with pain. This is not a termination of any sort for those souls—they just change schools, so to speak!

Souls choosing pain are very easy to identify. They progress more slowly with *much* more effort. Difficulties and discomforts abound and recede only at the last possible moment, when the person simply cannot take any more. At some point, the soul gets tired of the struggle; departure from the body often comes as a relief after a lifetime of strain. Some souls however, use painful growth in a more subtle manner. They *accept* the struggle and at times, even enjoy it. This is the highest method for achieving growth with pain, observable throughout history in the lives of many saints and spiritual leaders. This technique allows a soul to maximize the levels of pain they can withstand and growth they achieve. Embracing the pain provides a quality of transcendence. It still works, and some souls continue to use it. When you observe painful growth, allow yourself to see the good in it. Even though you intend to use growth with joy, accept the choice of others. *Everybody chooses growth.*

What's the Timetable?

Think in terms of cosmic time. A few years is just a blink of an eye from a cosmic perspective. Daily, you witness incremental changes in your personal energy and in planetary energy. The cumulative effect over years is clear and obvious, while each little daily movement is not so evident. Join us now to think bigger, longer and more expansively.

Planetary change is indescribably immense. Currently, transformation is moving very fast. This rate continues through the turn of the century, slowing a bit here and there for everyone to catch their breath. *This is a long-term situation.* One hundred years from now, the planet is a utopian place by today's standards! Fifty years from now, economic and socio-political changes are clearly underway. During the upcoming ten years, catalysts for change appear, instigating transformation at every turn. You lightworkers are the souls who plant the seeds of change that bloom in the next ten years! You must wait 100 years to harvest the fruits of your garden, but doesn't the harvest truly begin when the seeds are planted in the spring? With this cosmic timetable in mind, remember that *cumulative effort* is very important. Many, many small increments add up to massive quantities. This is the true strength of your group's effort: hundreds of thousands, even millions of souls—all making a simultaneous effort for an extended period of time. Your chosen work for this incarnation is not for one day, or even one year; it fills the balance of your lifetime! So, please take an occasional moment to think about the breadth of your group plan. Keep your focus day to day, but occasionally take the wide-angle view as well. It will refresh your soul.

Group Plan Update

Current planetary energies are triggering intense changes for many of you. Your lives are being restructured and remodeled to more closely fit the current status of your lifeplan. Changes in your daily life will occur as a result of your own *conscious* actions, but also by actions made without full awareness. Either way, you likely feel some pressure toward change. These cosmic "nudges" can be light or heavy, usually depending on your reaction; if you ignore a light nudge, a heavier one follows!

Information is the antidote we offer to alleviate any negative reactions you might have from this push into new territory. Humans are naturally inclined to remain in safe, predictable surroundings. Each of you has a different threshold for tolerance of change—the maximum amount of change you can adjust to before tension and fear are triggered. If possible, your Higher Self and your personal guides/angels accommodate your individual comfort level, while working to keep you on schedule and in place with regard to your lifeplan. If you understand where you are going, the adjustment to changing circumstances is easier.

Do you have any conscious knowledge of your personal lifeplan? If not, we advise you to seek out that information. This does not mean that you must go to a dozen different psychics to get a consensus opinion. We suggest that you look within *yourself* for this knowledge. Your guides provide the most appropriate descriptions and data for your current level of readiness. If you won't believe it, your guides won't show it to you! The full picture unfolds over time as your thinking expands to encompass the scope of your lifeplan. To get more details and clarity is to look higher, reach further . . . and *think* with an expanded perspective.

As the plan unfolds before you, every experience of your current incarnation makes sense, forming a clear pattern and design. The people and events of this life have molded you into a specific personality with a particular mindset; you shaped *yourself* for this plan over many incarnations, developing skills and abilities that may need to be reawakened.

For those of you in Wave One, your work has already started. All you required was the arrival of the new energy. For those of you in Waves Two and Three, your final preparation stage is happening now. For everyone, "team formation" is currently underway. Each of you operates on a particular "team," an interconnected group of souls who have made plans that interlock like puzzle pieces. As Wave One develops projects to a certain stage, their connections in Wave Two need to be in place to keep things flowing.

Considerable reshuffling and reorganization is happening at this time. There are souls who tried valiantly but will not arrive in time to play the first part of the game. Others are too spiritually injured to complete their part of the team's work. Some teams are missing players, while a few teams have basically fallen apart since only one or two souls arrived at the game field in good condition! Everyone who wants to play will have a position, but it takes extra time and effort to restructure. Look to your intuition and dreams to discover more about your team's day to day status. Even if your team is almost completely intact, team members must conduct "interviews" to fill even one or two openings. Such substitutions can require much readjustment, since each person brings very precise and specific skills to the game. All this interactive work is done on the astral plane while you sleep.

You may be asking, "Why are the plans in such disarray?" There are numerous reasons for so many souls to be having problems getting into their places on time and in good spiritual condition. Have you noticed that the Earth is bulging with souls at this time? As you might guess, everyone wants to be here to experience this truly momentous event, much like the crowd at the most popular movie or concert. This energy shift is the biggest cosmic event for many thousands of years! Even a short painful lifetime is a very popular "ticket" to get hold of right now. However, it may be difficult for you to comprehend that you are not really the audience—you are part of the show itself! Since many of your most trustworthy soul-companions are working on this project alongside you, the choices for parents who are "old friends" was seriously reduced. Many of you would normally have been parents to one another, rather than task companions. For this reason, a great many souls knowingly chose parents with whom there was an increased risk of childhood trauma. We are not saying these were "bad" parents, perhaps they're just younger souls with less experience, or erratic types who were unpredictable in their living skills (sometimes good, sometimes not so good). In any case, when some souls selected their parents/family, the best available options were less-than-perfect matches, but in a good physical location on the planet for getting connected to your group. (It can be difficult to get to Dallas from Sri Lanka by the age of 37, no matter how good your parents are!) The best available "seat" was obtained, for the overwhelming need was to get a seat at any price! In every incarnation, your soul takes some degree of risk in choosing those with whom you make agreements, because any cosmic contract can be abdicated or broken. Each soul who took a risk on parents or family members assumed that the group effort would enable him/her to complete enough speedy self-healing to get to their place on time. In some cases it worked, in some it did not. This is one reason for the surge in personal growth and self-healing in recent years. Many of you are very busy helping everyone you can get cleaned up for the big event.

All souls on the planet right now are making the choice between pain and joy. The sum of those individual choices determines the pathway of the planet itself. Every single person on Earth at this moment adds an incremental bit of energy "music" to the cosmic symphony coming from your planet. The White House group seeks to synchronize enough "energy-musicians" to draw the entire planet into harmony. The creation of a symphonic ensemble requires several stages of preparation. Each musician must do enough independent study at the elementary levels to achieve a moderate to high degree of proficiency. Of course, some musicians learn to play many different instruments (with varying levels of skill), and some players don't even choose their instrument until the last possible moment. The musicians gather in small groups to practice together—flute and piano duets, string quartets, opera soloists and their choruses. Then, the most chaotic time of all arrives . . . the entire ensemble begins to trickle into the rehearsal hall. Without knowing the exact layout, the various sections must find their places. The group must decide what songs to play, then practice begins in preparation for the concert. If there are imbalances, adjustments must be made. The disarray and confusion may lead to conflict and disorder. Problems must be identified and solved with compassionate communication. All musicians must be joyful, because JOY is the source of their "energy-music." You are in the gathering stage of your plan. The chaos is an expected part of the blueprint, but there is time allotted to fit everyone together for the big concert.

How can you be sure you're ready? Is there anything else you need to do? These are questions you must ask yourself. Do you have a sense of urgency about your personal growth? Are you feeling compelled to get your life in order? Use whatever energy methods or intuitive skills you have available to move into your particular seat in the ensemble. We cannot emphasize this point enough: *Get connected to your own higher guidance for daily assistance.* There is too much to do to be stumbling around in the dark! It is much less efficient to consult channels and psychics for information that will come *directly to you* with more depth and personal meaning. The increased energy makes the process of connecting to your guides easier than ever before.

Finally, on the subject of lifeplans: Think back to your childhood. What did you feel about your life, your reason to be alive? Did you sense a deep, inner truth? Can you find the sense of self you held before "being logical" and having "reasonable expectations" influenced you? Look around in your inner closets and see if you can find it again. Somewhere, you will discover your personal lifeplan—a treasure chest filled with plans for joyful growth!

Section Two

Personal Transformation

Chapter Six

You Are Involved!

Our goal is to synchronize all recipients of this information, so we will cover basic concepts quickly, then move into the more complex material. We begin with a single question which addresses the root of most metaphysical searches.

Why Are You Here?

We remind you that intense desire is required to enter the physical plane. Each of you are here by your own choosing, but the choice to experience life on Earth comes at a high price. The cost is *energy*. From a cosmic perspective, that is the price of all things. You sent out great waves of focused energy in order to manifest this lifetime, to be here in a physical body at this time. What could lead you to expend your energy toward that goal? The answer is simple. It is your preference, nothing more.

You may say, "But that is not so much! Isn't it something bigger, like a desire to return to Oneness?" The answer is the same, leaving the Oneness was your preference too.

At the core of all choices is one thing: *Preference.* If you seek to eliminate preference (as do some Buddhists), you exhibit a preference not to prefer, so you still have a preference! At the very crux of consciousness is the mechanism of preference. The ability to prefer is the essence of sentience. Higher levels of consciousness are achieved, not as you eliminate preference, but as you focus and extend it. Projecting ahead, seeking to pinpoint a laser beam of preference onto a distant and complex goal, indicates a high degree of preference ability. Complex preference improves the clarity and strength of soul energy, leading some to prefer existence as stars or planets. Others choose to experience group consciousness in plants, minerals and animals—or in collected energies such as our own. (We are an entity consisting of separate souls who have chosen to work together while maintaining individual awareness.) Multitudes of other choices exist as well. Consciousness that moves far from the physical plane has options that we cannot even explain to you. Since there is always someone preferring something new, there are unlimited choices within the Universe.

After leaving the Oneness, you preferred to align yourself with a "team," rather than move through the Universe as a solitary consciousness. Your next preference was in the selection of that team or family, choosing from many structures and shapes. Like us, you selected the "entity" approach, which maintains individuality without solitude. You may have assumed that all souls operate as you do, seeking to reunite with others of your group. Almost all souls on your planet are involved in this same preference for "entity" form, much like all teams at the soccer field are there to play soccer. There are many other configurations to choose from, however. There are a small number of solitary souls mingling with you "team players," but only a few.

We speak of this to alert you to the complexities of the Universe. Please understand the critical importance of *preference*. It is why you are here! As you access your ability to prefer, you improve your skill at achieving the life experiences you most want. Preference is more than manifesting, as it comes *before* manifesting. Magic happens when you establish preference. Preference is the highest act of consciousness, no matter what you choose to prefer!

How the Changes Feel

The condition of your planet reflects the sum of all preferences made by souls currently in physical form on the planet. Earth's reactions, such as an increase in natural phenomena like earthquakes and weather-related disasters, reflect the balance of all planetary energies. Such cataclysmic events happen in areas of the planet where there are large groups of negative, fearful people. Intensified energies promote a rise in human violence, on a nation-to-nation, as well as a personal level. Again, people living with fear and anger magnetize forms of violence to themselves. If you have a strong intention for *joyful survival*, intuitive clues will keep you safe. We recommend that you move through every day consciously and deliberately, paying close attention to your intuitive flashes. Do not bother with protective energy shields; they can draw to you opposing energies who will "push" on it. Remember to focus your thoughts on what you *do want* rather than what you *do not want*. For example, when you get into a vehicle, take a moment to visualize yourself arriving safely at your destination. If you pay attention, intuition will then guide you safely through any potentially harmful situations.

At the current time, your life is likely to be filled with strong lessons, with surges of personal growth for you and everyone around you. Issues that need work will come to the forefront of your experience. Intense feelings and situations may develop in your daily life, as this is how the Universe gives you "homework" and "final exams." Current lessons will intensify, or you may find yourself tested on how well you understand your recently completed lessons. One day you may feel quite tranquil and balanced, and the next you may suddenly discover buried or hidden issues coming up to be handled. For best results, use gentle, joyful techniques to finalize your lessons. Your goal is to extinguish the deepest of your negative thought patterns or fears, leaving a workable quantity to finish easily over the next few years. Your Higher Self "feeds" you lessons at the fastest possible pace you can handle.

New awareness levels of old problems trigger a need for personal growth and intensified inner work. When old issues are solved, new issues will arise. Over the next ten years, problem-solving continues, with your Higher Self directing the lessons for maximum efficiency and dharma. Because of your passionate desire to get to 100 mph, you may have lots of lessons "dumped" on you in a very short time. There is nothing "wrong" or "bad" about approaching the lessons slowly, but you have a *very strong intention* in place for getting to 100 mph quickly.

Try your best to recognize and finish with life-lessons as they present themselves. Your Higher Self feeds these lessons to you as fast as possible, in order to propel you toward 100 mph. If at any time you begin to feel overwhelmed, use your visualization skills to contact your Higher Self and your guides to request a slower pace. Imagine yourself talking with whatever "teacher" image you wish to create. Explain precisely what you need; the guide may simply agree, or the guide may offer an explanation which may help you stay with the accelerated pace.

It's fine to slow yourself down when you feel the need to do so. You should realize however, that although slower growth tends to feel more comfortable, it is possible to develop the skills to find JOY in accelerated growth as well. One of the keys to fast growth with JOY is a well-developed ability to problem-solve. (See Chapter Eight in this section, "School of Happiness" Problem-Solving Skills.) Another key to fast and joyful growth is the ability to use your intuition which is basically "tutoring" by your guides and your Higher Self. An expanded understanding of current events in your life gives you the perspective to recognize the lessons more quickly, while minimizing pain. In other words, if you can understand why you need a seemingly negative experience *at the time* it is happening, you can usually release the pain more easily. You can then move forward toward the positive outcome which is the greater goal. Be cautious whenever you enter the mode of *growth with pain,* for the discomfort will become intense very quickly.

Your lessons may jump from topic to topic in a seemingly random manner. Look for the underlying similarity in a variety of different situations that appear unrelated on the surface. When this happens, you have found a "blind spot," an incongruity in your belief system which influences your behavior in ways you no longer notice. If you can discover the common denominator, you can often speed up the process of concluding a lesson. Growth energy creates an environment for you to reevaluate such beliefs, deliberately and consciously.

What we refer to as "mutual growth interaction," is a commonly-used growth technique; a useful and efficient way for two people to share lessons. It occurs when two people interact simultaneously as student and teacher for one another. In this situation, you are compelled to behave in a particular fashion toward another person, who responds in turn with behavior that "pushes a button" of yours (hurts your feelings, makes you very angry, etc.). Your emotional reaction is strong, perhaps more intense than the situation alone merits. *Your response at this time is critical!* This is the perfect time to use some deliberate, newly-learned behavior to respond. That's the point of the entire interaction. Once you make a behavior change, your partner has an enhanced opportunity to develop a completely new reaction, breaking his/her own pattern as well. Be aware that old behavior patterns are likely to fail miserably. Take a little time to seek out a creative response, using all that you have learned over recent years.

Now that we have given you the "worst news" about your need to complete all those lessons quickly, here is some "good news!" With the new energy available, it is now possible to accomplish unbelievable changes in very short periods of time . . . *if you get aligned with positive energy!* Since this is such a critical concept, the next chapter provides a variety of methods to refocus yourself from negative into positive. Remember that fast, joyful growth is *always* possible.

The Team Needs You!

Remember that your group's plan is built of tiny incremental pieces. A mighty mountain peak erodes into grains of sand over time. In this same manner, you lightworkers intend to *build* a mountain out of tiny grains of sand! You may feel that one person's influence is imperceptibly small, but focus your attention to the individual's effect on the team as a unit. As you look around the Universe, countless examples bombard you which demonstrate how the "micro-world" provides the building blocks of the "macro-world." You are just one piece, but each lightworker is a magnet to attract more light energy to this planet. When you blend that light energy with the love energy natural to Earth, you exude a powerful dynamism—all by yourself!

Your job as a lightworker is to *be here* and to *feel JOY*. Whatever your lifeplan, it must bring you to a state of unparalleled happiness! You don't choose a lifeplan by spinning some cosmic Wheel of Fate; you choose what you prefer, even if that is now different from what you planned before this incarnation began! Your group plans require that everyone light the joyful spark within themselves. Find your inner spark and blow on it gently until it bursts into a lovely little flame; feed the fire with the fuel of JOY and see if you can create an inner bonfire! Light the way first for yourself, and your joy will then light the way for others to follow. JOY is not selfishness, nor is it vanity. JOY is your job. Get to work!

Chapter Seven

Flow with the Transformation

How do you recognize when you are in a negative energy focus? You feel it *physically*, right in the center of your solar plexus. It feels like a rock sitting there in your stomach. This sensation is a direct communication from your Higher Self, telling you that your thoughts *at that moment* are creating a future that you don't really want! The tension in your stomach may be accompanied by a tightness in the chest, which is a fear gripping you and blocking the energy flow through your body.

Don't be confused by emotions that are sometimes improperly labeled "negative." When expressed appropriately, anger and grief are useful emotions which will not trigger a "gut-message" from your higher guidance, nor will they block your energy. People who *never* seem to feel these emotions may have blocked anger or grief, thinking of them as "bad." These individuals have simply not yet learned effective and appropriate ways to express the darker emotions. At the other extreme, some people maintain a constant level of rage or grief. After a time, this seems so normal to them that all other emotions feel odd—even happiness! People of this type "forget" about an entire spectrum of pleasant emotional states, which limits their full range of feelings and energy.

Your goal is to feel and appropriately express *all* emotions. When you accomplish this, you become comfortable with both joy and anger. Truly negative thoughts and behaviors take you *away* from your lifeplan, away from your preferences. These negative thoughts actually create a future you don't want! Dark emotions, on the other hand, signal course corrections that are needed to help you stay on track with your lifeplan. For instance, grief indicates a termination of some sort, and time for a change; anger often signals an imbalance in a relationship or situation. "Shadowside" emotions quickly disappear when you acknowledge them and make the necessary course adjustments. Learn to tell the difference between your negative thoughts and your dark emotions.

How to Move from Negative to Positive

1. The first step is to *notice* that you are in negative. For many of you, the negative sensations are obvious and clear; awareness is easy. For others of you, however, negative is so common in your daily life that you no longer pay attention to it; awareness is the primary stumbling block. If needed, ask your Higher Self to intensify the "gut-message" to make recognition easier.

2. The next step is to *neutralize* the negative; you want to eliminate those signals in your stomach. It is very difficult to move directly from negative to positive. Just like shifting gears in your car, you need to move through neutral for a smooth transition from reverse to forward. When you ignore neutral, you risk damage to your transmission. You can use a wide variety of techniques to accomplish a smooth transition. A few examples are:

Take a walk.	Read a book.
Go to a movie.	Take a hot bath.
Take a nap.	Work a crossword puzzle.
Meditate.	Play or listen to music.
Clean your home.	Bake some bread.
Wash the car.	Pot some plants.

These activities share two basic characteristics: They occupy your mind and reposition your body. When your mind is otherwise occupied, you don't continue to think about your problem or situation from a negative point of view. Repositioning your body helps you to reposition your thinking as well. You are not ignoring the situation; you will return to it later with an empowered, problem-solving attitude, which requires a neutral to positive state of mind. If you are at work, or in a situation where none of the above techniques is possible, take action to disrupt your current negative thought pattern. Take a five-minute break or change to a more neutral task for a little while. Do not give your mind "free-rein;" focus tightly on whatever neutral activity you have chosen. At first, don't worry about feeling good, just eliminate the thoughts that feel uncomfortable.

Neutral is very powerful, but some of you really dislike using it. A sense of speedy movement is very "heady," even if it's going in the wrong direction! If you have trouble with frequent negative thoughts, you could be one of those people who like speed at any price. *At 90 mph it can be a very high price!* If you cannot get on track toward your goal, at least slow your movement. Neutral is valuable in that it keeps today's problems from getting bigger tomorrow. Worry has no value.

3. Once you achieve a solid state of neutral, use *creative problem-solving* to move into positive. A positive focus feels powerful and strong. You feel optimistic and hopeful when thinking about *solutions*, instead of problems. New ideas for resolving the situation come into your mind. You feel confident and energetic, ready to begin work with new clarity of purpose. Remember, within every problem and negative situation in your life is the opportunity to feel good *while* you solve it, not just *after* you solve it. Experience a few great solutions (not just compromises), and discover that creating joyful solutions is one of the pleasures of life.

Recognizing Lessons

The planetary energy transformation exhibits itself through astrological events, one of many influences. Certain planetary configurations trigger certain issues to come forward at certain times, magnetized by the planets involved. At times, these planetary influences may hit something within your personal natal chart which takes you by surprise. The root of the "surprise" is often a suppressed issue or a situation that has been in some sort of stalemate. The astrological configuration loosens the restrained energy, pulling forward something that is not in balance, capturing your attention. It is like a sudden gust of wind that blows open a door, knocking to the floor items which were in a precarious balance on the edge of the table. Then, just as quickly, the wind dies down, leaving you to sweep up broken glass or restack the pile of letters and magazines cluttering the floor. Valuable and efficient lessons come about when you observe what has "blown in" with these winds. It might be as small as leaves or as large as tree branches; as small as having a "bad hair" day, or losing your car keys, or as big as having your car stolen, or receiving a call from Publisher's Clearinghouse that you won a million dollars! Unexpected surprises are part of the new, faster energy, so don't worry about predicting what will come. Be flexible, relax and try to enjoy the surprises. Sometimes the unexpected can be fun!

People tend to ignore issues that come up repeatedly, waiting until something big requires them to work harder to correct an imbalance. It is like a car that sputters and chugs along day after day, not in good shape but still running. Some people won't put that car into the repair shop until it stops completely! Intensified planetary energies cause your personal growth issues to bloom, large enough to capture your attention. As you work on negative thought patterns like self-deprecation or arrogance, circumstances may strongly trigger those feelings more frequently and with more intensity. If you ignore a negative atmosphere at home or work, your need to make a choice to stay or leave may suddenly be intensified by changes that escalate the situation. Depend on some kind of "winds" to blow through your life over the next few years.

How can you best deal with the "winds" of change?

1. Tidy up the precarious things in your life *before* they get blown to the floor and broken. If you quit ignoring problem situations, you won't need unexpected surprises to bring them to your attention.

2. *Look closely* at whatever "blows in," because lessons tend to be completed once you understand them. Watch for repetition; this is a sure sign that an issue is stuck in a stalemate. Whatever lessons come into your life, start work on them right away. The more you procrastinate, the more difficult things will be. Even a small amount of attention is hugely effective in reducing your potential for discomfort. Neutral energy alone won't facilitate your progress on lessons very much. Move *very quickly* from negative to neutral, then keep going steadily into a positive perspective as you seek to understand the situation and develop your response.

How Change Happens

Every growth surge has a similar form, the core structure of how souls tend to learn. This is a "scientific function," based on how energy is transformed through growth. Right now, the entire planet is involved in a massive synchronized growth surge, the systematic formula for which applies to individual spiritual evolution as well. The explanation that follows is true for the planet in a macro-cosmic sense at this time, but it's also true for each individual soul in a micro-cosmic sense. Even after the planet's energy shift is complete, souls will use this same system with every personal lesson.

In growth, consciousness has a bell-shaped curve; there is low level of consciousness of the lessons at the early and late phases, and higher awareness in the center of the experience. Don't be mislead, however. A great deal of energy transformation happens during the beginning and final phases of the learning curve. There are three main phases you move through in any personal transformation:

✧ *Phase One.* Most of the energy changes are at the subconscious level. People with very well-developed intuition have some sense of the movement. During this time, souls are drawn into situations that provide needed lessons. Often, the learning situation comes in the form of some new person or relationship which enters your life. For example, a romance may begin or a new person may be hired at work. Phase One provides the foundation for personal growth that comes later. Although events may seem insignificant at this stage, this phase is critical in "creating the lesson." No growth can occur without a catalyst. There is a high degree of "blindness" at this stage because if you could see what was coming, you might try to evade the lesson. Sometimes, you may observe other people, friends or family, who move blindly into an obvious "train wreck" from your perspective. Be patient, for often they are within this phase of the growth curve. Who knows? You may be doing the same thing in some area of your life, just as blindly!

✧ *Phase Two.* This is the phase of conspicuous growth. What was subconscious in Phase One now becomes conscious. Most people clearly feel a sense of working on lessons. There are obvious problems to be solved, things that are difficult to ignore. People in this phase can usually tell you precisely what area of their life is "under construction." It is vital within Phase Two to neutralize negative thought patterns while using creative, positive thought to manifest solutions and goals. Some try to block the shift into Phase Two by refusing to acknowledge the problem, but denial will only escalate the pressure to move forward. In order to evolve more smoothly, try to recognize the lesson as early as possible. Notice whenever a person or situation starts to bother you—maybe just enough for some internal "grumbling." This is a clear indicator that a small lesson is underway, or a bigger lesson is in its early stages. The sooner you tackle the work, the sooner it will be complete. Watch for patterns created by many small lessons of the same type with different people; this is a sure sign you have a larger issue hiding from view beneath these small matters.

✧ *Phase Three.* The personal growth work during this phase moves back into your subliminal thought processes once again. In Phase Three, you blend lessons learned recently into your overall pattern of behavior. You are "recalculating" all of your internal belief systems against this newest set of formulas for living. At times, your internal work creates a "test" of the most recent lessons, particularly when the new beliefs clash with some deep, old, opposing thought patterns. You may find yourself busy redoing lessons you thought were completed long ago, because more recent lessons disclosed some flaw in the old solution. This phase is very tricky, because you may suddenly plunge into work on old issues which seem completely unrelated to recent lessons. Do not discount the immense value of this stage of the process, because it creates congruency among all your belief systems, and your belief systems are the basis for your behavioral patterns. When belief systems are incongruent, you may find yourself frozen, unable to take action or make a decision. The "computer operating system" of your spirit simply shuts down until the computer program is cleaned up again. The energy of this phase creates a system of "perpetual growth," as recently completed lessons trigger new lessons. The end of one cycle is the beginning of the next cycle.

Getting in the Flow

The new planetary energies create physical reactions, too. Since your body is responding to massive surges of energy, your physical condition may fluctuate from one day to the next. Try to remain flexible with your schedule, allowing yourself to ease up when you feel tired but compensating by extra effort when your body feels energized. This type of "high/low" in personal energy is a permanent component of the energy shift. If you learn to listen to your body, there will be an improvement in your overall productivity. We understand that not all of today's employers will want to follow your individual physical schedule, but this will become more and more a part of how things work over the next 50 years. At this point, try to accommodate your personal energy state whenever you can as you make plans and schedule your activities of all types, both work-related and personal.

Earlier, we mentioned astrological influences. You will deal with uncommon astrological energies for a long time. These unusual planetary influences are one source of the shifting of the planet's energy. It may be helpful for you to learn a little more about what astrological events are expected in the next three to five years, including how these will impact you personally. The most important part of these upcoming years is to develop a sensitivity to your own internal energy. The ability to monitor your own reactions *while they are still internal* is very important. If you recognize energy changes in yourself, you can make adjustments and rebalance your energy before "blasting" the people around you with an energy surge. In addition, you can pull up your own energy level when it gets low without consciously or unconsciously absorbing energy from the people around you.

The source of many interpersonal problems is a lack of balance in one area or another. It's possible to reduce your external difficulties a great deal by analyzing all difficult relationships and locating the area that lacks balance. No matter which planets are impacting your personal energy, you can make corrective adjustments to your own energy to compensate. The process is similar to what you do when you drive an automobile–look at the road, look at where your vehicle is heading, make an appropriate correction with the steering wheel; repeat the sequence over and over and over again. Constant monitoring is necessary, but it need not take over your life. As with driving, adjusting your personal energy can become a sort of "automatic system" that does its work while your attention is simultaneously on other activities.

Internal energy flow is clearly affected by the type of energy that flows into your system. This is being radically changed at this time, so please be patient with yourself (and others) while everyone learns how to manipulate this new energy. Energy blockages are more apparent, requiring internal work. At times, these blockages cause energy to pulse out of your system in an imbalanced way, clearing constricted energy. This might manifest as an angry explosion, a crying spell, or even an illness. We suggest that you pay attention to this energy while it is still internalized, reducing the need for such manifestations.

The critical point here is that you must take responsibility for your own energy, even when it pulsates higher or lower than normal. If you "blame" the planetary influences for your erratic feelings or actions, you will receive lessons to help you reestablish personal responsibility. Responsibility lessons are often tough and painful. The most efficient way to maneuver through these energies is by observing your personal energy carefully, noting what response you get from others, and seeking to determine where the boundaries are in every relationship. In the next chapter, we discuss this topic at length through a concept called the "Power Aura." After some practice at identifying boundaries, you develop a strong internal image of what balanced and harmonic boundaries are like. When you can recognize them, it becomes much simpler to stay within the harmonic boundaries–even when other people do not. This is your goal for handling your own personal energy.

Chapter Eight

School of Happiness

Happiness in life is not luck or fate, it is a skill. This chapter deals with how you can learn to achieve happiness while living out your lessons on the physical plane. There are a variety of skills required for happiness; as you develop these skills, you extend your own self-love and the love you offer to others. You can find on what level of happiness you are currently working by asking yourself this: In what area am I having difficulty right now? The skill levels for happiness are:

Level 1   Communication Skills

Level 2   Relationship Skills

Level 3   Problem-Solving Skills

Level 4   Decision-Making Skills

Level 5   Skills for Managing Abundance

Level 6   Leadership Skills (includes Teaching and Parenting)

Level 7   Flow Skills (Expanding your Capacity for Joy)

Our primary reason for creating this "school curriculum" is to help you to perceive happiness as a learned skill. In the future, your planet will teach these in school classrooms beside math and science. Instructing children in happiness skills, presenting concepts along with plenty of experiential opportunities, allows youngsters to grasp the cause and effect of personal actions. Once an individual discovers the power of his/her choices and actions, a sense of personal responsibility and high self-esteem is the natural outcome.

Happiness skills influence all spheres of your life—work, family, friends, and play. You move magnetically into situations providing lessons in the skill areas needed to complete your lifeplan. The first three levels are basic skills which create a good foundation for the others. As you achieve acceptable skills in these basic areas, your lessons move into the higher levels. For example, what if you have problems with abundance, specifically, a lack of money? Lightworkers for the most part, do not want large amounts of money to deal with *until* they have achieved good skills in the basic areas *plus* skills at managing the abundance, too. You lightworkers intend to use money energy in totally harmonic ways, having already experienced the misuse of money and power in previous lifetimes. If you lack the most basic communication skills, such as the ability to say "no" to an inappropriate request, you will not allow yourself an excess of money to be mishandled. Whenever you feel blocked, be sure to look into more basic areas to see what might be needed.

In spite of what we just said, you do not really work at completing the levels in order. The most efficient manner to "graduate" is to move from level to level, constantly expanding all the skills in a balanced fashion. Happiness skills are best gained in a "revolving" manner, rather like tightening the lug nuts when changing a tire on your car; you move from one to another, escalating the overall level each time around, instead of working on one level all the way to the end.

We remind you that the ultimate goal of the physical plane is *experience*—of all kinds, not just joy. Each lifetime is like a science experiment, undertaken to find out "what happens if . . ." After hundreds of lifetimes on Earth, you now seek to tighten the focus of the experiment, intending to achieve speedy growth with joyful experiences instead of painful ones. Do not forget however, that painful experience is also valid. Others around you are choosing it every day. Your current goal is to convert painful experience into something equally effective but more pleasant. Your experiment in "spiritual alchemy" begins with yourself; transform the painful areas of your life into joy. We offer this information to help you in this goal, but each person chooses between pain and joy without losing the *experience* from a lifetime in physical form. If people around you choose pain, remember that a painful lifetime still fulfills the soul's desire for experience. Happiness skills also provide experience, *WITH JOY!*

Level 1: Communication Skills

Communication has many facets. While working on these skills, you may want to isolate a particular topic for further study. Entire books are available on some of these individual subjects, so look for ones that attract your interest or fulfill your need. Communication can generally be categorized into two main skills which can then be broken down further into particular sub-skills. The main ones are:

✧ How *Others* Communicate (Good Listening). This area focuses on all the interpretive skills you use to improve your understanding of people as they communicate *to* you. It includes perception of verbal communication as well as nonverbal things: body language, voice quality, male/female communication styles, etc.

✧ How *You* Communicate (Sending Clear Signals). The focus here is on you and your skill at communicating your meaning clearly and precisely. If confusion is your daily companion, this is a good topic to look into. Learning to communicate well may include the practice of techniques such as learning to say "no" in a harmonic way, speaking the hard, unspeakable truths, expressing anger appropriately, or using "straight talk." (There is a great book entitled "Straight Talk." See Recommended Reading list.) You may need to learn more about asking good questions or about the magic of using the truth (gently), instead of telling "white lies." When communication is blocked, your emotions deposit themselves within your body; you may need to learn more about how your own body communicates emotions to your consciousness. In addition, many layers of inner communication go on inside your head, like old "tapes" from your childhood which influence you internally and probably influence your communication with others as well. You initiate improvements and control changes in yourself, so work on this area usually creates tremendous results.

We have some specific suggestions for how to achieve better communication skills:

1. *Seek clarity in all your communications.* Everyone can improve in this in some way. Are you frustrated by interactions with others who seem to confuse things at every turn? These people provide you with opportunities to try new ways to *clearly* communicate your comments or wishes. If you can interact cleanly with those people who are fighting it, you can certainly interact smoothly with others like yourself who seek clarity. As you improve in this skill, notice improved clarity in your *inner* processes as well.

2. *Cultivate an experimental attitude with changes in your communication.* Since human bodies have a built-in resistance to abrupt or extreme change, you can create problems for yourself by trying to change habits overnight. You see, speedy change tends to be more from growth with pain; but the

movement is often erratic—three steps forward, two steps back. Growth with joy is generally slower, but very steady and progressive. If your negative communication habits are based on self-protective behaviors developed in childhood, your entire system needs time to see how safe these new methods of communication "feel." Once you have proven the effectiveness of a method by experiencing harmonic outcomes and positive emotions, the old habit becomes easy to extinguish in the excitement of a newly-found self-empowerment. In other words, when you try something new that works great, you automatically feel stronger and better about yourself. In that state of mind, change becomes joyful.

3. *Write down your thoughts in a journal.* This is particularly helpful as you seek out the negative inner messages you habitually repeat to yourself. Just seeing your thoughts in writing prompts an instant "reality check," because their childish roots become very evident. The journal serves several other purposes as well. It allows you to monitor your growth over time, as you go back and reread old journal entries. A journal provides a place to "think aloud" to yourself, to process a particular issue as you consider a behavior change. You can create and practice new communication behaviors through writing, jotting down several possible ways to express something. Additionally, written communication is often an effective way to deal with people who do not listen well; the person has a letter or memo which you both can reference to check his/her understanding of your message. A journal helps you polish your skills at writing with clarity. Over time, using a journal helps to clarify *internal* communication as well, with the added benefit of improved outgoing communication.

4. *Carefully observe what happens when others communicate.* You can complete important lessons by making deliberate changes in your own communication techniques, but you can also gain a great deal by using neutral observation. By this,

we mean observing communication between people in situations which don't trigger strong emotions in you. This might be people at work, or casual "eavesdropping" in public places, or even watching movies and television. While observing, look for what *does not work* as well as what *does work*. Let others demonstrate for you what are clearly ineffective methods, and save yourself the energy expended on unsuccessful methods.

5. *Notice discrepancies in communication.* As your skill at reading people develops, be sure to notice people whose words don't match their body language or their actions. Observe that whenever there is a discrepancy, the person's true feelings tend to match the body language/action rather than the words. Reading a person's true intent and feelings is a basic skill needed in problem-solving and decision-making, as well. Observe carefully, and consider testing your observations for verification.

6. *Learn how to gently speak the truth at all times.* This is a very important skill, for nothing has more power than truth. We don't mean you should "dump" truth all over others, unasked. Find something true you *can* say, rather than speak an untruth. People always sense deceit anyway. Improved intuitive abilities make lies even more obvious now, as well. Inner clarity cannot exist in the fog created by deceit, so start *inside*. Usually, this means you need to develop ways to say those "hard truths." You can say almost anything in a gentle and loving tone of voice. Experiment with this and other methods to work out useful techniques for loving honesty.

Level 2: Relationship Skills

The core issue of this entire level is personal boundaries. While living in human form on the physical plane, you are at your most isolated as a soul; other levels of consciousness provide for more fusing between souls than is possible for humans. This is the source of much frustration, but it also triggers great leaps in spiritual growth. Physical isolation is part of the physical plane; it pulls each of you into a search for more connection and spiritual blending. The intense separateness of human existence is not found on any of the other spiritual planes you frequent. We wish to make this very clear, because many of you have forgotten why you feel such loneliness and detachment. The isolation of your physical form provides intensity; it is a highly concentrated form of your individual essence. The physical plane *requires* physical boundaries. In the areas of feelings and personal power, however, you need technical skills to maintain good personal boundaries. This is a primary lesson, required before unconditional love is possible. These boundaries are not limits that confine you, and they are not barriers to keep others away. We define good personal boundaries as *harmonic limits to personal power and personal responsibility.* You are responsible for your own feelings, but not the feelings of others. You need to live your own share of life, but not anyone else's share. Easy to say, but not so easy to do!

The Power Aura

Generally, an aura is defined as the radiant energy around a physical form, visible to those with the ability to see energy. Power Aura refers to one particular spectrum within the aura as a whole. For those who can see auras, the Power Aura is yellow. Depending on your way of viewing auras, you might need to "change channels" to isolate the Power Aura. It is modulated through the Third

Chakra. (If you are confused by any energy terminology used here, refer to Section Three, Chapter 12, Energy Basics.) It is not necessary to see auras to work with the Power Aura. You need only visualize it (picture it in your mind's eye), making size adjustments as needed. The Power Aura is a glow of yellow light surrounding your body. It may be so flat that you can barely see it; it may be as big as a room. Use of the Power Aura provides you with a simple, non-judgmental way to observe and adjust your interactions with others. Instead of trying to change and monitor each daily action, you can work from the energy level and set your Power Aura at the desired size.

Humans strive for *contact*. Touching personal energies is the most intense form of contact available to most humans. (For those with special energy skills, other types of contact are possible, but most people are working on getting their energies to touch.) Once you understand that humans are seeking to "rub their Power Auras together," you can then make sense out of some odd human behavior. Why does an abused woman stay with the husband who beats her, even at risk to her life? Why does a man intensely pursue a woman, and then drop her once she falls in love with him? Why do some people (male or female) always fall in love with the most emotionally unavailable person they can find? Why do so many adults have difficulty dealing with their parents? Why are two-year olds so hard to handle? When observing the Power Auras in these situations, you set aside judgement of who is "right" and who is "wrong." You can perceive the relationships as pure energy, and make desired changes from the energy level.

Here are some examples of different types of relationships and what the Power Auras might look like in their interactions:

Strangers and Acquaintances: Both people in this relationship have flat to moderate Power Auras, so that nobody touches anybody else. In public, it is generally accepted to "pull in" your Power Aura. Even so, you will often notice people with an air of authority or importance about them; these people have more Power Aura "sticking out." A police officer, for example, often needs to do this. Usually, as two people move into a friendship, their Power Auras will subtly expand until some boundary is created.

Bully/Victim: The Victim has a very flat Power Aura; the Bully has a large Power Aura. Don't be fooled by the names, as both individuals share equally in creating and keeping this type of interaction. The Victim feels the Bully is the only type of person he/she can get really close to. Others with small Power Auras do not "touch" the Victim. The Bully has found someone whose aura doesn't resist, which feels more comfortable than the constant power struggles in the rest of his/her life. For both, this relationship is a "perfect fit" which works until the Bully inevitably pushes beyond whatever small aura the Victim has. In childhood, the Victim never learned how to extend the Power Aura safely. The Third Chakra may be significantly closed off, restricting the energy flow available to boost the Power Aura. Even if the Victim gets the energy out into the Power Aura, further expansion of Power energy is blocked by the habitually over-extended Power Aura of their partner, the Bully. Both lack the ability to adjust the boundary of their Power Auras.

Chaser/Runner: The Chaser and the Runner have the same type of Power Aura; both simultaneously seek and fear having true contact with another person, but each is in a different phase. The Chaser has a Power Aura that expands only until it touches someone, then it retreats back into the smaller "safety zone." The Runner stays in a defensive posture, with the Power Aura pulled back but ready to expand if nobody is pursuing. When these two types come together, a perfectly balanced "dance" occurs as they exchange roles and chase each other back and forth. Another shared quality is that both have very frail Power Auras that cannot withstand any pressure from another aura; these people know how to move the aura in and out, but they don't know how to safely hold a solid boundary. If cornered, the Runner may "pop" his/her aura out suddenly, pushing others away. This action creates enough space for the Runner to escape, on the run once again. Chaser/Runner relationships are highly volatile, but can be very satisfying to those who are fearful of true energy contact. This system creates a tantalizing illusion of intimacy, while maintaining the "safety zone." For those who wish to make a true energy connection, however, this pattern is tiresome and quite uncomfortable.

Parent/Child: Generally, the Parent has a slightly larger Power Aura than the Child. At times this may be reversed, with the Child controlling the Parent. An infant usually has a small Power Aura which, over time, grows in size as the baby learns independence skills such as walking and talking. At two years old, the child's Power Aura expands markedly in a very short period of time. Often, the aura gets bigger than the child can handle, but it's important not to compress the aura too much or the child may never get comfortable with handling a "normal" size Power Aura. As the Child matures, the Parent's Power Aura is slowly and gently pulled in, allowing the Child to slowly and gently learn how to handle more and more of his/her own energy. In general, conflict between Parent and Child reflects the constant renegotiation of boundaries as the Child grows up. By "conflict," we simply mean disagreements and negotiations, not necessarily arguments and fights. If there are no differences *at all* however, everyone may be using flat Power Auras and there is probably very little true emotional contact. Ideally, the Parent and Child will achieve well-balanced energies which often touch pleasantly. If an adult Child and the Parent revert to the childhood Power Aura shapes, stress will occur in their adult relationship.

There are more variations than these, and you may also discover combinations of the above patterns. In addition, you should not assume that the relationship style will necessarily fit the names above. For example: a mother/son relationship may follow a Chaser/Runner pattern, or a husband/wife relationship may follow a Parent/Child pattern.

Level 3: Problem-Solving Skills

This level has three primary skill areas to develop. Remember that both Communication and Relationship skills will also be involved. Each of the three skill areas are equally important. Do not get stuck by ignoring any one area. Problem-solving requires a "double perspective," meaning that you think about a long-term goal (5–10 years from today) at the same time as the immediate future (tomorrow). Good problem-solving combines opposites: right-brain/left-brain, masculine/feminine, focused/spatial, change/stability. The easiest way to create solutions comes from "opening" your mind and your emotions, broadening yourself to wider degrees of understanding and possibilities. Good abilities in the following three skills are needed for problem-solving:

1. *Define the problem clearly.* This is the skill most ignored in the problem-solving process. Obviously, there is great difficulty in truly eliminating a vague, undefined problem. Over 90% of the time, humans spend masses of energy "solving" issues that are secondary to the core dilemma. This is inefficient and wasteful of energy. (Remember dharma is your goal!) Time spent diagnosing the problem is very productive. While in a neutral state, all involved parties discuss the difficulty in great detail. Each person needs to describe *precisely* what they experience. Questions should be asked until each person has a true understanding of what the other experiences. If the discussion turns into an argument, drop it for the time being. Get back to neutral, review some basic communication skills and try again later. Each person should make observations about themselves only! This eliminates "attacks" that trigger an argument. Sentences can begin with phrases like "When (this or that) happens, I feel . . ." Sentences should *not* begin with "You always . . . " After sharing both/all "sides" of the problem, your goal is to state the

problem without laying blame on anyone. Create a statement that is completely neutral. (e.g. "We disagree completely on how to spend money.") Now, go one step further, because your true problem is usually deeper. For instance, money and sex problems are almost always power struggles at the core. Some other common "core problems" are trust issues (fear of abandonment) and control issues (fear of losing yourself). This exercise is like tilling the soil for your garden.

2. *Find and define a mutual goal.* This is a critical part of the problem-solving process. Accomplishing this step is not difficult to do, but it can be difficult to remember to do it. You must discover and state the mutual goal. If you cannot find an area of mutual agreement, there won't be a solution that is mutually satisfying. Most of the difficulty in developing this skill comes from how most humans "see" things. People notice only the differences between people, sometimes incorrectly assuming that other areas not discussed are in agreement. Often, the mutual goal is found in the long-term future, with the problem itself creating short-term interference. By intentionally stating the mutual goal or solution (and not just the problem), energy is directed from the negative to the positive. This is the transformative point. It plants the seed of the solution in the tilled soil of your garden.

3. *Create and test a mutually satisfying adjustment to the situation.* Most people try to jump directly to this part of the process, suffering a bewildering failure because they do not even *know* about the first two skills. Many psychological and energy changes occur during the first two steps of the process, so a solution built without them as a foundation will be weak. When you define where you are now, then state where you want to go in the long-term future, the best pathway will appear as if by magic! Yes, you will need to make changes in order to "walk that pathway," but a truly perfect solution will energize you! Don't be satisfied with a simple compromise.

Expand your thinking in order to get a great, creative solution. Good negotiation skills are needed, but the very best solutions are great ideas that come in a flash. Usually, the best solution requires a change in some basic format or system. Test the potential solution so nobody feels constrained. An experimental attitude provides needed flexibility. "Grow" great solutions in your garden!

Harmonic solutions are difficult to express in general terms, so we offer some examples below.

Problem #1: A 13-year old girl clashes with her parents almost daily over money. Daughter wants expensive designer clothes, with no regard for budget. Mother and Father must unhappily say "no!" to these emotionally-charged requests. Constant arguments disrupt the family, as Daughter constantly asks for lunch money, movie money, and pizza money. The "hidden" problem is a combination of power struggle and control issues. The daughter's behavior signals that she is ready for more power and more control over her own life.

Great Solution: Daughter is given a *firm* monthly budget from the parents, which she may spend in any way she wishes. The budget includes lunch money, money for toiletries, entertainment, and clothes. Special items like a winter coat or a special occasion dress are negotiated, often with the parents paying half, over and above the budget. Daughter gets her own checking account to learn about banking. (Note: This doesn't work with weak boundaries. The parents *must* be able to see her "suffer" consequences, like when she has no money left on Friday night for a movie.)

Outcome: Much fewer arguments about money. Parents can count on steady monthly expenses. Daughter learns to budget her limited resources; she begins avidly watching sale ads in the newspaper for the first time. Daughter is proud of her grown-up independence, and she proudly shows off her checkbook to her friends. Parents notice their daughter adjusting her behavior as she experiences the consequences of her choices.

Problem #2: A married couple is struggling with their relationship. She tends to "push" him—craving more conversation, more emotional sharing, seeking more intimacy. He retreats, tuning her out by reading the newspaper, watching sports on TV, and woodworking in the garage. The more she pushes, the more he retreats. It's getting worse each day. She picks fights with him just to get his attention, while he tries to ignore her anger. The "hidden" problem is a complicated mix of power struggle, control, and trust issues.

Great Solution: They schedule a weekly "intimacy meeting." She must restrain from pushing issues at him all through the week, saving them up for the meeting. He must spend a little time through the week preparing for the meeting, trying to notice his feelings and figure out a way to express them to her in any way he wants (not just words). These are not "bitch sessions." Problems may be aired, but in a problem-solving way. *Feelings* are to be the focus. Imaginative methods of communication are highly-recommended, since good communication involves more than just talking. He must push forward a little; she must pull back a little. Balance and comfort are the goals. Each feels the other is making some effort toward a solution, which improves trust.

Outcome: At first, time is spent negotiating solutions to little problems, but the meetings soon evolve into something both productive and pleasant. Over time, the couple discovers that more intimacy comes naturally when they communicate in creative ways. One week she ends the meeting with an "exotic dance" to express that she would like him to pay attention to her. One week he reads her a wonderful poem that he found at the library, expressing many of his feelings about their relationship. She learns about other methods than talking to communicate; he learns it's safe to communicate his deepest feelings in whatever way he wants. After several months, the planned meetings subtly shift into an unplanned, natural flow of intimate communication. Both are much happier.

Level 4: Decision-Making Skills

When confronted with two or more options in behavior, you have a choice that requires a decision. You make thousands of small and not-so-small decisions every day. Obviously, some individual decisions have more impact than others, but some seemingly trivial decisions grow larger through repetition. Most people spend a lot of time making "big" decisions (like who to marry or which house to buy), but may give little attention to the small daily decisions (like how much to eat, or whether to smoke a cigarette). When these little choices build up and accumulate into a problem, it can be hard to connect those small decisions with the larger problem. Anyone who smokes cigarettes, or consistently under- or overeats is choosing to ignore this kind of pattern.

Your first job is to realize that *everything* in your life, large and small, is the result of decisions you have made. If you still believe that your life is controlled by something or someone outside yourself, you will have difficulty making conscious, deliberate choices.

We cannot emphasize this enough . . . EVERYTHING IS CHOSEN.

You choose your parents, your birthday, your body type, your birthplace. More importantly, your choices have lead you to this time and place, to your job, to your financial status, and to your health. Note: The only exception is when karma is involved. We define karma as any time a person takes choice away from another person, and this creates a karmic "ribbon" that must be "untied" by repeating the original action in some way that replaces choice. It is not so common as you might think, and very few circumstances in your life are based solely on karma. You make many choices consciously, but a large number are made from subconscious preferences and assumptions "programmed" by your Higher Self to help you achieve the overall plans for your current lifetime. We recommend that you connect with your Higher Self in order to understand the larger context of your decisions. If you see "the big picture," you can operate more deliberately. We are *not* talking about making your decisions on intuition alone or logic alone, but a combination of the two.

Let us describe the structure of your consciousness, for using it effectively improves your decisions. Your physical form does not hold within it everything that you are; it is simply too much to handle in the tight focus of the physical plane experience. Your consciousness has two primary components—*will* and *memory.* The consciousness in your body holds approximately 90% of your will, which is your capacity to prefer one thing over another (commonly called desire). The other 10% remains with your Higher Self on the Astral Plane. The reverse is true for memory, as your current body holds something less than 10% of all experience (depending on how much conscious recall of past lives you have). Your Higher Self holds most of your memory, which can be accessed to regain lessons and experiences from previous incarnations. Your memory also holds the blueprint you created for this lifetime, the agreements and plans already in place for NOW. If you operate without a strong connection between these two components, your decisions will lack effectiveness. You do not want to be directed completely by your Higher Self, for it has very little of your will; however you do want to make use of past lessons you've accomplished to smooth your current pathway. For this reason, we recommend that you deliberately access your Higher Self when needed, much as you would use reference material from a library. There are three component skills which facilitate appropriate decisions and choices. They are outlined below, and we have included corresponding exercises for you to try:

1. *Ability to Connect Past, Present and Future.* In order to plan and choose well, you must be able to see how the seeds planted yesterday grew into today's garden. The same skill allows you to predict what today's garden will look like when tomorrow arrives. This may seem very simple, but many of

you have difficulty in this area because of emotional blocks (rather than cognitive blocks) such as anytime you do something that is obviously unhealthy for your body, but satisfying to your emotions. You know better, but may convince yourself that "just this once" it will be okay; repetition over time then accumulates into a big problem. If you have trouble figuring out how you got into a predicament, you probably need to work on making these important connections. The seeds of the situation were probably planted long ago and, since people tend to follow previous patterns of behavior, most will repeat the same mistakes over and over. To those of you who can see the patterns, repeating the same errors like this seems very strange. Remember that someone who has disconnected the past from today will not connect the present to tomorrow either. When fear rules the ego, it does not allow a person to remember errors, or to use that information to improve decision-making. It is very normal to eliminate painful thoughts from your mind; the conscious mind simply "erases" the connecting thought process, alleviating the pain but leaving a person to repeat a negative behavior pattern.

Exercise: Think of a relatively small mistake you made recently, something that doesn't trigger inner intensity for you. Ask yourself this question: "If I could do this over again more perfectly, what changes would I make? What outcome would I prefer and how can I accomplish that?" Practice this thought pattern with small issues, gradually increasing the intensity of the problems. Over time, you will develop comfort in looking at your errors in a productive way. You are retraining your ego to make the connection between action and consequences, particularly negative ones.

2. *Ability to See All Possibilities.* When you feel powerless and unable to decide something, you may not be looking at all your choices. This is a common problem for "victims" —people who don't like where they are, but who are unable to see a doorway out. If you have an area of your life where you feel

victimized, you will usually find the solution to the problem *outside* your current options. You may have dismissed some good alternatives based on erroneous beliefs. If you believe something is impossible, it becomes exactly that; if you open up your belief system, you expand your options. For some, a lack of flexibility causes the choices to narrow. If you have trouble with change, you might ignore a good option out of resistance to all change, even good change! All restrictions to your choices come from fear. If you eliminate fear, your menu of choices expands dramatically, and your problem-solving abilities are also enhanced.

Exercise: Using a simple decision you make every day, list *all* possible choices without limitation. It can be a silly decision with as many ridiculous answers as you can find. Some possible topics to consider are: ways to position food on your plate, ways to get from one room to another, ways to kiss, ways to show affection for someone else. Consider trying this exercise with another person, comparing ideas. Try this exercise with a child; you may see just how "stuck" in routine adults tend to be! (It's fun, too!) Once your list is complete, spend some time expanding it even further. This will demonstrate to you how many more possibilities there can be when you make a conscious effort to find them.

3. *Ability to Adjust Short-term Behavior for Long-term Consequences (Cohesive Behavior).* If you tend to act for immediate reward only, you will have difficulty matching your daily behavior with your long-term goals. The problem is not a lack of self-control, but an inner conflict that is played out through actions that lack cohesiveness. Decisions from day to day which don't "match" indicate a need for work in this area. A person with conflicting internal belief systems often engages in self-sabotage behaviors. This person chooses daily behaviors which alternate from one goal to another, resulting in erratic movement through life. The most common conflict is between short-term rewards and long-term goals. Children

learn this from choices like "Do I buy candy today or save up my money for a toy?" The solution is to *connect* the short-term behavior to the goal, in order to maintain motivation and focus on the long-term.

Exercise: Select an area of your life where your daily actions conflict with a long-term goal—consider looking at a habit like smoking, overeating, or overspending. Create a visual image of the long-term goal. Add emotion to the image like how comfortable and happy you feel when the goal is reached. Hold this image for a minute or so, intensifying the good feeling in your body. Notice what part of your body feels the best. If you don't notice any particular spot, use your stomach area. Mentally shift the visualized image from your mind *into* that body part. Now, whenever you notice that good sensation there in your body, you know your behavior is on target toward your goal.

Level 5: Skills for Managing Abundance

Many of you are currently working on this skill, wondering why you cannot improve your finances more quickly and easily. The block is often insufficient competence in one or more of the basic Happiness skills, particularly in the Communication and/or Relationship areas. For example, if you are unable to say "no" to others when appropriate, the Universe may say "no" to you! You created this protective mechanism to keep you from wasting or misusing large sums of money, for you have already done that in earlier lifetimes. If you believe this to be the source of your abundance problems, get to work and improve these fundamental skills. Please realize that lightworkers require superb skills in all areas to complete lifeplan activities, so you cannot settle for average skill levels!

Abundance levels tend to match *perceived* need levels, which causes a feeling of scarcity. An old saying goes, "Work expands to fill the time available." With money, the saying might be, "Spending increases until it depletes bank accounts available." Similar energy systems are at work in both situations. At this time of consciousness expansion, a more precise illustration could be made by adding a word to the beginning of each saying: *Non-deliberate* spending and *non-deliberate* work are more exact descriptions of the current concept. Clear intentions provide power to all actions, whether you are "spending" money energy, time energy, or work energy. Evaluate how "awake" you are as you expend energy in any form. Are you using your intuition, your logic *and* your conscious will to make deliberate choices about how to spend your energy? If not, try to do so. For more efficiency, seek balanced interactions.

For our purposes, we define *abundance* as a feeling of *plenty*. When you have abundance in your life, you feel you have enough (and more!) of *anything* you need or want. This is a broad definition; it includes money, work, play, health, intimacy, sex, comfortable surroundings, clothing, free time, fun, etc. Begin by developing a picture of what abundance means to you personally. Your first discovery may be that you need to adjust the image you hold to a more realistic perspective. We are *not* saying "Think smaller." Think as big as you possibly can, but try to imagine the reality of the experience. The purpose here is to understand that a "price tag" comes with some types of abundance. If you want to be rich and famous, do you feel ready to lose your privacy and anonymity? Will you wonder if people like you because of who you really are or because of your money and fame? Get specific about dollar amounts and how you would invest it. How much income per year feels abundant to you? How many dollars in a savings account would make you feel that you have plenty? What do you need in any area of your life to say, "*I have enough!*" The core question here is this: What is plenty to *you* and what preparation do you need to handle the abundance?

If you lack abundance in any area of your life, you have located an area that needs preparation and work. Abundance is often symbolized by the "Horn of Plenty," representing the harvest of fruits and vegetables from the garden. If your garden has not been prepared with tilling, fertilizing, the planting of high-quality seeds, weeding and watering—how can you be surprised when you get only a few scrawny plants and lots of weeds? If you can determine what work is needed to plan and prepare your garden, you are ready to see speedy results from your labors!

Many of you suffer an insatiable neediness for tangible objects (like houses, automobiles, clothing, etc.) This comes from scarcity in some emotional area of your life (often fear of abandonment) stemming from your childhood experience. A well-meaning parent who entangles showing affection with giving objects may be a source for this condition. The objects you need so urgently are symbolic of the unconditional love that you truly crave. *Need* is different than desire; need has a desperate quality, signaling that fear is the source. Need works like a hole in the bottom of your "energy-bucket," never allowing the energy to reach the top and flow over the sides in true abundance. As long as you *need*, you will never have enough—no matter how much you have. Many, many wealthy people do not enjoy their wealth because needy feelings drain away their sense of abundance. If you find yourself constantly craving *anything* (money, objects, food, alcohol, etc.), evaluate the energy source of the feeling. Using visualization, take a look at your internal energy system and try to locate the empty spot that cries out in hunger; typically you'll find it in the stomach and/or the chest areas of the body, near the third and fourth Chakras. Self-esteem issues are the most common source of this craving sensation; lack of self-love and/or lack of self-power are usually at the core of neediness. Once you visually locate a "black hole" (an area without an energy glow), imagine the spot filled with sparkling energy pumped in from the surrounding areas.

Others of you experience your lack of abundance differently— more happily; you may have a sense of waiting for it to reach you.

Abundance is necessary for all you "racers" who intend to reach 100 mph. How can you be happier than ever before in any lifetime, without a complete sense of prosperity? Each of you included a way to achieve abundance within your blueprint for this lifetime. For some of you, there is a feeling of comfortable anticipation for that time to arrive. (Some of you are a little less patient!) If your abundance skills are working fine, you may simply have to wait out a timing glitch. Returning to our garden metaphor, even the most well-prepared, hardworking gardener must wait for harvest time to arrive. Completing your plans, while becoming prosperous along the way, helps to create the inner joy that propels your energy above 90 mph! You have delayed some of your abundance to appreciate it all the more.

All abundance is some variation of basic energy. Money, love, creativity, power—all of these are energy interactions. You improve your ability to manage abundance as you learn more about how energy behaves. As you open yourself to stronger energies, you move through various skill levels and lessons. If you turn away from a particular issue, it will return with another "face" but with the same underlying issue. Abundance lessons are usually very practical, having to do with daily choices about "real world" situations rather than starry, other-worldly things. For this reason, some spiritual teachers disdain concerns about abundance. We do not, for it is the most concrete and measurable application possible for your energy skills. If any area of your life is in disarray, including your finances, you will not be able to achieve 100 mph.

Bear in mind that you will generate *tangible results* as you bring abundance into your life. Some of our methods for improving your abundance management skills may seem particularly "nonmetaphysical." You are existing as part of the physical plane, and we highly recommend that you keep a significant proportion of your focus there rather than continually seeking to move beyond the limitations of physicality. When making decisions on how to handle your abundance, your most effective method is to blend a harmonic mixture of intuition and logic. Use your logic to gather information and create a group of possibilities. (e.g. What are my investment choices? What return/risk quotient comes with each choice?) Next, use your intuition to expand or refine those actions. (e.g. Do I get a "gut feeling" for any of these possible choices? Do I get an intuitive sense to keep looking, a feeling the list isn't complete?) Now, go back to your logic to verify your intuition. Continue in this manner until you find a solution that "feels" right and "thinks" right, meaning that your logic and your intuition are both satisfied.

As you might guess, there can be lots of work and study involved as you gather and verify your intuitive choices. For this reason, we have several recommendations for how to develop your abundance "muscles." Like working out with weights, you need to create an individual program and work at your own pace.

1. *Know your current financial status* (whether it is healthy or not). Can you balance your bank accounts? How much money do you owe? Are you spending more, the same, or less than your current income? You must be willing to acknowledge your current position in order to plot movement to another location.

2. *Learn about tax planning.* Your accountant can only fill out the forms according to the way you decide to distribute the money. There is a great deal of self-empowerment when you know how to plan your spending for maximum tax savings.

3. *Observe your shopping and purchasing style.* Are you logical or emotional? Do you plan ahead or do you buy spur of the moment? Experiment with different styles to see how they feel. Try going to the grocery store without a list compared to going with a list. Your goal is efficiency as well as good feelings. It's possible to teach yourself a new style, if you wish.

4. *Use observation and intuition to discover profitable businesses.* Notice how they operate and what they feel like. You are learning how to select *highly* profitable stocks or other

investments, and also how to adjust your own business or job so it is a magnetic, high-energy zone that attracts customers and profit.

5. *Look for interesting books on business and money management at the bookstore.* Two possibilities to consider: *More Wealth Without Risk* by Charles Givens provides specific, practical advice on money management and investment; *The Great Boom Ahead* by Harry S. Dent, Jr. describes the coming economic conditions of which you are preparing to take advantage. Notice that the economist author dedicates the book to a spiritual master.

Level 6: Leadership Skills
(including Teaching and Parenting Skills)

In many ways, this level is the most difficult yet rewarding skill area for happiness. As you might guess, your lifeplan requires that you develop strong abilities in this area. However, many of you plan to be involved in situations that don't look like the Western definition of leadership. You may need to work on one or more of these areas, so use your intuition to guide you about where to begin. We remind you here that the first five levels of Happiness Skills provide a strong base for these higher skills, but that lessons seldom come to you in this exact sequence. Work on whatever lessons you find right under your nose, for those tend to be the most needed; use your intuition to determine where to begin.

Leadership. This can mean to go first and bring a group behind you, or it can mean to send people in the direction of your choosing, as you point the way. Both of these techniques have value, but current planetary energy makes the first method more efficient. It is difficult to *push* unless you use fear, while *love* works well as a magnet. If you go first using love as your bait, those following you automatically have a focus on the positive. Feminine leadership techniques tend to work best right now. While these have been used extensively in the Far East, most of you in the Western world do not recognize these techniques as leadership. They may seem mysterious and odd to you. Viewing Eastern leadership through the lens of Western society beliefs can make it difficult to tell who is the real leader!

Here is what Eastern leadership principles teach: A good leader uses power gently and as seldom as possible. Allowing the natural order of things to flow provides natural consequences, which a good leader harnesses to his/her higher purpose. A good leader keeps one eye on the larger goal, the long-term effects, and the group as a whole. Gentle well-placed nudges from a good leader are sufficient, making heavy domination unnecessary. A good leader seeks to understand the cause for each effect in order to create the desired consequences for the group. The true leader is not just the person with the title, but rather the one who influences the outcome.

As you can see, there are many nuances and subtleties to Eastern or feminine leadership. Unknowingly, you may have been working with these issues for quite some time. We recommend that you look around for the areas of your life where leadership operates. You may be leading one person (your child) or you may be leading an entire group or organization. We are *not* suggesting that you abandon all usage of masculine-style leadership; we *are* suggesting that you extend your skills by adding on an additional layer of leadership methods and techniques. You need both styles for your work, but be prepared for tremendous results with little effort when using the feminine leadership style at 90 mph!

How do you recognize when you are working on leadership skills? What forms do leadership lessons take? You may be surprised at the life lessons that fall into this skill area. Following are broad descriptions of some of the many ways leadership lessons appear in your life:

✧ Anytime you have difficulty with authority figures or "rules," you strengthen your self-esteem and inner will to become a better leader. At some point in their lives, all leaders turn inward for moral guidance rather than looking outward. Many "difficult" children grow up to be strong leaders; others may be docile as children, but face a confrontation with authority at some point.

✧ When you find leadership thrust upon you by others, you are being handed opportunities to practice and improve your leadership skills. Whether it is the PTA or a large business project, you are "rehearsing" for later leadership. Take the reins and drive the wagon as much as possible. If one leadership method doesn't work well, try a new one. The point is to get you to try out new leadership behaviors and techniques.

✧ If you have a child, you are *definitely* working on leadership skills! If you have a child who is a leader, you have taken on a particularly complicated project! You are shaping those who carry your work into the next phase, those who will some-day take your lightworker inventions and make them an everyday part of life on this planet. While Henry Ford's generation invented the automobile, it was the next genera-tion that built the superhighways and added power steering. It is during your children's lifetime that your White House projects will become "main-stream." Parenting leadership may be one of the most important but overlooked areas of leader-ship, but many of you plan to focus heavily on this skill. There are a tremendous number of powerful Old souls currently entering Earth's physical plane as children. Look around for one (or more) near you. You can knowingly guide them as they seek to reach adulthood with good happiness skills of every kind.

✧ Involvement with conflict is another source of leadership les-sons. When you find yourself in the middle of a conflict, especially if the difficulty is primarily between two parties (people or groups), you are in a situation that provides an opportunity for you to experiment with various new methods of leadership. For instance, mediation is an extremely important leadership skill. It utilizes all of your happiness skills, improving as they improve. If a reliable old technique suddenly quits working, don't throw it out of your "toolbox." In the long-term, you need to use every tool you have, but these short-term lessons "force" you to find or create some new tool, thus adding to the old ones in your toolbox. Just because you only need a screwdriver for a particular job, don't throw out your hammer!

✧ Leadership through teaching has many uses, and many sources for lessons. Effective salespeople are actually teaching by answering questions and providing information to their clients. Good healers and counselors also teach through their work. Business executives and managers lead effectively by teaching their employees more efficiency and basic happiness skills such as Problem-Solving and Communication. Most teaching leaders use a combination of *instruction* (information provided at appropriate intervals, combined with experiential learning opportunities) and *modeling* (effective behavior from the leader which serves as an example after which the student may pattern his/her own behavior). In your daily activity, observe what you are teaching others through instruction or modeling—whether you are conscious of it or not!

What Kind of Leader Are You?

Ask yourself a few questions. Our intention with this "quiz" is to provide you with a map of your true leadership abilities. Many of you are better leaders than you give yourselves credit for!

Do other people come to you for advice and counseling? Do people tend to "gather" around you and follow you like sheep as if you're the shepherd? Do friends/family occasionally remind you of something you once said or did that really made an impact on them?

Have you ever found yourself talking to a total stranger about their deepest feelings or biggest problems? Do you have strong opinions about social and political issues of the day? Has anyone ever told you they wanted to be like you? Has anyone ever seemed to strongly dislike you for no apparent reason? Do you dress to follow clothing trends or do you wear whatever you like? Have you ever spoken to a total stranger in a book or video store to offer a suggestion? Do people in public places come up to you asking questions about where to find or how to do something?

If the answers to some or all of these questions is yes, then you exude some intangible quality called *leadership*. People respond to leadership energy without consciously knowing why. People may be drawn toward your energy—asking you questions, telling you their problems, sometimes trying to give you *too much* power over their decisions!

When you come across someone who seems to dislike you for no apparent reason, it's likely that they are working on a beginning level of leadership. They are reacting to your leadership energy with an unconscious desire to resolve the hierarchy, like stags battling for herd dominance by crashing their antlers together. For the most part, you will not find it helpful to engage in the battle with these souls. Stand aside or ignore their combative behavior if you can.

Leadership energy is the purple hue within the rainbow of colors in your aura, modulated through the Crown or seventh chakra (at the top of your head). This energy is quite different from the yellow of the Power or third chakra, however the two are closely related and are most efficient when used together. The seventh chakra is sending and receiving during good leadership intervals, providing intuitive information between leader and follower. This psychic link fuels the interaction. When you sense a need for leadership energy, open the seventh chakra. As you intuitively receive needed information, your action (or non-action) pathway becomes obvious to you.

Level 7: Flow Skills
(Expanding Your Capacity for Joy)

In previous sections, we discussed tangible behavior modifications. This topic is very different from the other six. The primary feature which sets this level apart from the others is this: *Flow* is not an action or a learned behavior . . . it is a state of being, a mindset, a deliberate focus which transforms any action or behavior into a joyful experience. As we move into a more complete explanation below, please keep this distinction in mind.

What does *flow* mean? For our use here, we mean a state of Oneness with the Universe. This state of mind increases joy, creativity, self-empowerment, and total involvement with life. Oddly enough, when you are in the flow state, you lose the sense of isolation characteristic of the physical plane. You merge your energy with your surroundings. Fear and negative thoughts fall aside as outwardly-focused concentration pulls you out of the ego and into the flow of consciousness.

Autotelic Experience

Re-experience for a moment those times in your life when you felt most alive. Countless situations provide the trigger for peak experiences—a child's first smile at a parent, a sailor holding a tight course into the wind, a musician creating a new song, a child breathlessly placing the final block on a toy tower. These moments occur at unpredictable times, even in the midst of crisis or danger. Some people court danger on race tracks and mountain peaks in search of this optimal sensation. A struggle which forces you to meet a challenge of any sort can lead to such an experience. A comprehensive look at this topic can be found in a book entitled *FLOW: The Psychology of Optimal Experience—Steps Toward Enhancing the Quality of Life* by Mihaly Csikszentmihalyi.

For ease of understanding, we'll use the same terminology as this author, who labeled the flow state an "autotelic experience," and the person who enjoys them frequently as an "autotelic personality." The word "autotelic" derives from two Greek words, *auto* meaning self, and *telos* meaning goal. Autotelic refers to a self-contained activity, something that provides its own reward in the act of doing. If you do something with the expectation of a future reward, it is not an autotelic action. If you do something because you enjoy doing it, you can create an autotelic experience. It is possible to integrate autotelic episodes into every aspect of your daily life—at home or office, playing soccer or raking leaves, singing or sewing. Your goal for this lifetime is to learn how to bring joy into every moment of every day—*to EXPAND your capacity for joy.*

What are the common elements for most autotelic experiences? In order to learn how to shift into the flow state as often as possible, you must clearly understand the necessary components. Following are several elements common to autotelic events. *All* need not be part of every optimal experience.

- ✧ Activity that provides both challenge *and* requires skill. (Notice that most enjoyable experiences provide this naturally—games, crafts, art, music, dancing, reading and even socializing!)
- ✧ Intense concentration. (Irrelevant information is excluded, which removes negatives from consciousness.)
- ✧ Merging of action and awareness. (Person becomes one with activity.)
- ✧ Clear goals and feedback, creating complete involvement. (Provides a sense of forward movement.)
- ✧ A feeling of general well-being with a powerful sense of control.
- ✧ The loss of self-consciousness, a lack of self-scrutiny or self-judging.

✧ The transformation of time. (Sometimes fast, sometimes slow, the event creates its own rhythm.)

✧ The sensation of increased energy *flow* throughout your energy system. (The basis of all the other elements.)

You need not develop proficiency in all other happiness skills before beginning work on this level. As you increase your autotelic behavior, you bring more high-grade energy into your system which creates rapid growth in every other area of your life. Flow leads to improved relationships and choices as your energy pulsates strong and clear. Remember, *flow is a state of mind that leads to enhanced happiness.*

Increasing the Frequency of Flow Experiences

Yours is a highly personal journey, with countless ways to enter the flow state of consciousness. Begin by figuring out what triggers the flow state for you. Bring flow into other activities by creating challenges, goals and feedback. Try attaching "games" to work activities not normally considered "play"—like a family contest at raking leaves, or for one person raking alone, rhythmic designs or music coming from the look or sound of the leaves as they are moved. Of course, you will have your own preferences as you create energy patterns that you enjoy, but here are some broad-based suggestions for increasing your flow experiences:

1. Use one of your five senses to attach your attention to one aspect of an experience. This trigger (sense) becomes the focus of your goal and feedback loop. If you have trouble finding a trigger, shift from one sensory mode to another. For example, you may discover an auditory trigger (crunching) to induce the flow state in an oral exercise (eating cereal). Ultimately, you may discover that one of your five senses is stronger than the others, which helps as you add more and more flow events to your life. With practice, you can grow in your ability to use multiple senses simultaneously.

2. Set a clear goal for yourself in the selected activity. Many
    pursuits have natural goals. For instance, reading the first
    page of a new book immediately establishes a natural goal of
    going to the last page of the book. In some cases, the lack of
    flow is caused by the lack of goal. Your goal can be anything;
    it can be as simple as JOY, created by combining words and a
    melody together for a silly song in the shower, for example.
    An important aspect of an autotelic personality is the high
    level of self-esteem that results from large numbers of suc-
    cesses and goals reached. A habit is created, a habit of choos-
    ing an objective and reaching that objective by personal ef-
    fort. Choose goals that require some effort, while remaining
    within reach. Goals chosen too low will induce boredom; too
    high will cause anxiety. Flow lies in a balanced place be-
    tween these two extremes.

3. Build a "flow loop" within your activity by adding feedback
    to your goal. The goal pushes your energy outward; the feed-
    back completes the loop, pulling the energy back to fuel a
    stronger surge of energy on the next action. Successful at-
    tempts or close-but-not-quite attempts can fuel a stronger sec-
    ond try, since a desire to improve is strengthened by either
    outcome. For example, video games have a natural "flow
    loop" in their structure. Knowing this makes it easy to un-
    derstand why they have such wide popularity.

4. Remember that your only limit is your creativity. The only
    things absolutely required to establish flow consciousness are
    mental focus and the shaping of data into a pattern. For
    example, you will never achieve flow while playing chess if
    you don't learn the rules of the game. Flow occurs as you
    concentrate your attention and establish a non-chaotic mean-
    ing which attracts even more focused attention. Meaningless
    information swirls around you all the time. You create the
    flow state by discovering meaningful patterns in the data.

5. Observe children, particularly young children, to see natural
    flow energy at work. Whenever you tell a child to "go play,"
    you are really saying "go flow." Everyone uses flow exten-
    sively in early childhood, for this is how so much learning
    (crawling, walking, talking) happens in such a short period of
    time. If you have trouble reconnecting to the feeling of flow,
    try some of your favorite childhood activities. In some cases,
    a low challenge level may make it boring. (It's harder to color
    inside the lines at 4 years old than 40 years old.) Some may
    be more challenging now than they were then. (Those little
    jacks and tiny ball are harder to handle when your hands are
    bigger.) Some may stay just as exhilarating as ever. (Almost
    everyone likes to see how high they can swing.)

Seeking Joy in Everyday Things

This section is an added corollary to the flow information.
We often mention far-reaching lifeplans and complex group agreements, but your life will never be truly and completely *joyful* unless
you learn to achieve joy in small daily activities. Remember that
you lightworkers intend to build mountains out of the tiniest grains
of sand! Like most people, you spend your days preparing meals,
eating them, chatting about daily events with others, feeding the
dog or cat, reading the newspaper, watching television, taking a
shower, making the bed, paying bills, mowing the lawn, driving to
work, buying groceries, cleaning the toilet, answering the telephone,
working at your job. This is your challenge—to turn each of these
activities into a *joyful* experience. Here are some suggestions on
how to accomplish this goal:

1. *Immerse yourself in the activity.* Whenever you choose a
    particular activity, do it with complete focus of attention.

Notice details. Tune in with all your senses, observing everything around you carefully. Experiment with different and interesting ways to go about the activity. Don't let your mind wander. Keep it on the activity at hand.

2. *Become more skilled at the activity.* Improve your efficiency and creativity in every activity you undertake. Even the most "boring" of jobs can be reworked for more efficiency. Some activities can become a huge source of improved self-esteem if you challenge yourself to new levels. Cooking is a good example of this.

3. *Turn the activity into a game.* Add some low-level competition. If others are involved, it's more game-like if you compete. If it's a solo activity, you can compete against yourself. Remember that all flow activities have some sort of challenge involved. No matter what the activity, you can concoct a way to make it a friendly contest of one sort or another.

4. *Ritualize the boring activities.* There is intense power in repetition; this can be observed in the rituals of many organized religions. Repetitious activities can be exceedingly boring unless you allow the repetition to create a transcendent energy, taking personal energy into a higher state. By "ritualize," we mean to give each part of the activity a meaning that elevates the actions. It is not necessary to make a religious connection, but some kind of spiritual meaning is often helpful. (e.g. While planting flowers, take time to "talk" to each individual flower—perhaps give each plant a blessing for growth.)

5. *Add music or rhythm to the activity.* Music pulls you quickly into a timeless consciousness. For hundreds of years, humans have added music to repetitious or boring activities. Examples of this are old-time songs of the railway workers and the singing cowboys alone on the range. Military drills have long involved chants and songs. "Whistle while you work" is an age-old way to help you be happier at a mundane

job. Listening to the radio does not usually achieve your goal here. You don't want to be pulled away from the activity, but further *into* it. Listen for the natural rhythm or sound of an activity; sometimes birds singing or leaves crunching for example are enough to induce the flow state. Other times, you might join in with music of your own kind.

6. *Be fully in the moment and fully in your body.* You may discover how much of your day disappears when you aren't there. When you are thinking of last week or next month, you are not fully in the moment. When you get "into your head" too intensely, you are not fully in your body. For maximum joy, you need all parts of yourself—mind, body, soul—to connect in the same place at the same time. Often, this is most easily attained with comfortable daily activities. As you develop more awareness of "getting yourself together," you will find this important connection easier to maintain.

As lightworkers, achieving personal happiness is your job. It is your reason to exist here on the physical plane. Grasp your lessons and embrace them, for they attract cosmic light-energy into your body. Each skill you develop, each lesson you complete, each difficulty you successfully resolve is another light bulb in your personal light show. When you lightworkers reach 100 mph using Happiness Skills, this planet will look like a cosmic version of "The Strip" in Las Vegas—countless individual lights all shining at once in a glorious display!

Chapter Nine

Protection Against Yourself

Do you understand and agree that a soul chooses every experience? If not, you will have great difficulty with some of the information that follows. You may need to check into this concept and rethink your basic beliefs. How tough to accept that hard lessons appear in your life by your own choice! How easy to give up responsibility for your life, then relax and gripe about how terrible things are! Of course, all the thought energy focused on negatives will bring you even more terrible things to gripe about . . . and a spiral into growth with pain has just been created. By you, of course.

Self-Responsibility

Self-Responsibility is a difficult concept for some people. From a metaphysical standpoint, this means that each person is responsible for creating his/her own reality. Why then, do so many people give themselves such harsh lives? Once you accept the concept of self-responsibility, you must look into how you create your own problems. You can learn how to stop making your life so hard!

We understand that this is not an easy subject. There is something enticing about the victim role, the martyr role, the righteous role. The battles you fight in life are poignant and romantic. Enemies and fear are very compelling. As long as you need protection from anything or anyone outside yourself, you continue to cling to a belief that you did not choose this! But, you did. As you enter the path of the self-aware and self-directed soul, observe that you need only protect yourself from one source of pain . . . yourself.

As guides, we have some difficulty explaining the subject of self-responsibility. We are not interested in providing ways for you to beat up on yourself by describing where you are messing up, making errors, or doing a bad job. We do not want to give you additional reasons to be hard on yourself. We *do* want to facilitate your growth by pointing out useful possibilities, but you must choose what to try in your life. Just as we are not responsible for your problems, we are not responsible for your solutions. Remember, once you accept full self-direction, you get more than the blame for the so-called "mistakes." You also get full credit for the successes.

Self-Observation

Most humans find it easier to love others than to have self-love. With this in mind, please use self-observation gently. The main objective of self-observation is to identify aspects of yourself which block your progress and subsequently, that of others. As you expand your own self-love, you simultaneously expand the love energy sent out to other souls. Agape, or unconditional love, must first move into your system on internal circuits of self-love. If these pathways are small, the entire agape system remains small. Expand the internals, and the externals also enlarge, which in practical terms, means this. . . *you can only share that which you own.* If you do not have unconditional love for yourself, you cannot offer it to another soul. As you gather up self-love, you then have agape to give freely to others.

Self-Healing

As a corollary to the idea of self-love, *you can only heal that which you love.* If you desire to heal yourself (physically, spiritually, emotionally), you must develop a truly self-loving attitude. Once you "own" that self-healing energy, you have tremendous healing energy to offer to other people, even to the planet. There is a three-stage process for self-healing.

Stage 1. Decide on the number one problem. Choose a single issue for which you will actively seek a solution. Selection of one problem at a time eliminates the "problem list" and helps you keep a sense of perspective and power. When you layer problem upon problem, you develop a sense of hopelessness and futility. Establish your focus on the primary issue, even if another problem keeps coming to mind. You will not ignore the other issue for long. You must simply tighten your perspective in order to create a bite-size piece to chew on!

Occasionally, there is a recurring secondary problem. If another issue persistently returns to your thoughts, one of two things is likely: You need to change priority of the issues, or the two are connected in some way.

State the problem clearly to yourself. Write the problem on the top of a blank sheet of paper. Use neutral language and take care to describe the issue without putting yourself down. (e.g. "I have a problem handling money. There is an immediate problem this month, but I want to create a long-term solution as well.") If the neutral language you've used to describe the issue sounds odd to you at first, it may be because you are habitually critical of yourself. Your neutral statement has removed the guilt and shame to which you've grown accustomed. You now embark on a new pattern of thinking which breaks that old habit.

Focusing on a primary issue is a key part of self-healing. Don't worry about selecting the "wrong" problem. Whatever you feel compelled to work on is a problem, and any problem you solve helps you feel better! Your goal is to create a solution to today's most irritating problem. Eventually, you will solve them all. Here are some questions to ask yourself as you single out a problem:

✧ What am I most worried about right now?

✧ What am I thinking most about?

- ✧ Is this connected to another deeper issue that I'd rather avoid?
- ✧ What is the worst possible outcome?
- ✧ Is there a time issue with this problem? Do I need to hurry or slow down?
- ✧ Is this someone else's issue that I've taken on as my own?
- ✧ Is this a short-term problem, a long-term problem, or both?
- ✧ What is causing me the most pain and fear right now?

Plan to deal with the chosen issue for a short time. If you find yourself stuck after a full week, choose another problem. It may be that the first one is no longer a primary issue, or perhaps you need to work on a related problem first. Don't stagnate. You need not stick with your primary problem until it's completely solved. It tops your list only until you get a good solution to test. Keep this in mind as you make your choice; go ahead and tackle the big problems—one at a time.

Stage 2. Create a menu of solutions. Whether you are seeking to make a major life change (e.g. stop smoking; turn in your resignation at work), or are looking for experimental options—things to try once or twice (e.g. show more assertiveness at business meetings), your goal is to recognize and list all possible *solutions.* Write them on the same paper on which you stated the problem. At this point, don't concern yourself with judging the value of each solution. List as many possibilities as you can, even those you're sure you don't want. A vital part of the process happens here, as you observe one problem with several possible solutions. Put your creative mind to work. Sleep on it at least one night, since this gives your Higher Self an opportunity to send in ideas while you sleep. Put your "solution page" near your bed, maybe even under your pillow!

Stage 3. Choose a solution and outline a plan of action. This is an exercise of your personal power. Making a conscious choice requires an act of deliberate will. As you develop your skill at choosing it gets easier and more fun, too! Use a combination of logic and intuition to guide you, and expect some magic at the moment of selection! You feel powerful when you make a good choice. When you declare, "I choose this!" you are no longer a victim. If you're nervous, choose one of your potential solutions to experiment with; or select your favorite two or three, and plan a way to test each of them. If needed, create other lists to supplement your thought processes such as pros and cons or projected consequences for each experimental solution.

Complete these processes in writing, particularly at first, because it allows you to observe how your mind operates. Additionally, you will have a record to review in case you return to this problem another time. In fact, you may find it helpful to have a written record of your experimental solutions too, successful or not! Sometimes the solution you resist the most turns out to be the most effective. Once your problem/solution list is complete, you may clearly see that there is no other workable solution; you may discover the true lesson hidden within the situation.

With that in mind, consider writing down what you believe is the lesson to be learned from this problem. Once you realize what the lesson is, the solution is always close at hand. Sometimes the problem disappears as soon as you figure out the lesson behind it. Each problem you have is simply a lesson waiting to be learned, a puzzle to be solved. It comes back over and over, until you figure it out and deal with it!

Self-Sabotage

As you accept full responsibility for your successes *and* your difficulties, you quickly begin to wonder, "Why am I so hard on myself?" The following three beliefs trigger self-sabotage behavior (and we offer corrective measures for each):

1. *You give yourself exactly what you believe you deserve and nothing more.* If you lack self-love, you never allow yourself

to have all you want in life. If you accidently find yourself succeeding and moving above the limits you created for yourself, you will find some way to knock yourself back down to the "comfort zone." This happens out of a self-protective fearfulness that tells you to move back to a safe place before someone else knocks you back. This reaction is common in people who have *love* entangled with *esteem* or *value*. From somewhere, you have developed a deep belief that you must earn love and appreciation and/or you must deserve affection. This form of self-sabotage is extremely common in romantic relationships—individuals who only seem to date people who treat them badly, but justify it with, "I know he (or she) is a jerk, but least I know what to expect."

Correction: Challenge that self-limiting belief with information. Do you love only those who "deserve" it? Do you feel closer to someone when they constantly adjust their behavior to earn your love? Notice how affection works toward and from pets. People seek unconditional love. Do you have an internal image of what unconditional love looks and feels like? Try to create a picture in your mind of what agape is like in action. Give yourself a new goal to work toward by clearly defining love to yourself in this way, whether it is love of self or love of others.

2. *You fear the consequences of success more than the consequences of failure.* For many people, success carries with it a burden or a price. This may be an expectation from others to maintain some high level of operation, or it might be a buried belief that all good things that come to you have a price tag in pain of one sort or another. Evaluate your deepest desire, looking for some consequence of it that you find unappealing. (e.g. Fame means a loss of privacy and the possibility of public criticism. Anonymity might not be your goal, but it feels safer to you, so there you stay.) The unknown causes fear, creating a huge block to your progress and holding you in the "known," even if you don't like it!

Correction: To unblock yourself, adjust your thinking on the subject. Figure out what you need to learn to feel comfortable with success. Try learning more about how some well-known individuals have happily dealt with fame. Your goal is to reduce or neutralize your fears of the consequences of success, using information as the tool.

3. *You enjoy the feeling of overcoming difficulties, so you create many problems for yourself to overcome.* If you believe that a hard-won victory is of more value than an easy one, you may be creating challenges for yourself to sweeten your feelings of success. Are you constantly solving the same problems? Do you enjoy telling others about the challenges that you have recently overcome? People with this self-limiting belief recreate old lessons, especially ones that have long been completed. You do this to create a superficial sense of achievement, without actually venturing into new territory. Frustration at the beginning of a problem quickly shifts to joy as you peel away each layer of difficulty. Problem-solving invokes strong feelings of inner power and strength. These feelings are helpful and valuable, often increasing your self-esteem. However, you use a tremendous amount of time and energy by working this way. You always have plenty of new problems to deal with, do you not? It's time to stop repeating old patterns.

Correction: Evaluate the problem areas in your life. Recognize that the same difficulties keep recurring, even though you know exactly what to do when they come along. Restructure your thinking by gathering more information about the primary issues of your life. See how you feel if you consider making bigger changes, working out effective long-term solutions to the problems that you keep rehashing. We are *not* saying that you should invoke fear reactions by making massive changes in the short-term; we *are* saying that you will enjoy a sense of achievement when you truly conquer an issue, particularly if you must stretch and grow to do it. The key is to expand yourself into new territory, even if only for an experimental solution. You'll begin to perceive the difference between true growth with forward movement versus superficial growth which is like jogging in place.

The three self-limiting beliefs above have a common source: Fear. In your search for growth with joy, you need not use fear in any form. Fear sometimes blocks your progress completely; this is usually quite obvious. Fear can merely slow your progress at times, however, and this can be much trickier to discern and release.

What changes will allow you to think more about your goal, and less about whatever blocks you from that goal? You may have an automatic thought response, connecting every thought about your goal with a matching negative thought about why it's not likely or possible. How can you disrupt that pattern? Some suggestions are:

✧ *Write down the goal and the opposing thought(s).* Evaluate each negative, determining a course of action to minimize or eliminate it completely. Now you have extended the thought loop from positive/negative back into positive. If you cannot stop the automatic negative thought, you can recover by taking the next step, that is creating *another* automatic thought . . . a positive response which eliminates the block. For example, if the initial thought *Boss* triggers an automatic thought *Jerk!*, then complete the thought loop with a solution thought *Send Energy.*

✧ *Learn how to break automatic thought loops.* First observe the pattern by figuring out what negative internal "tape" automatically plays in your head. In order to disrupt the pattern, you must first recognize it. Similar to the last idea, the technique is to establish code words to set up a new chain of thoughts. For example, in your old thought pattern, *Money* triggers *No money,* consciously change the pattern so *Money* triggers *Enough money.* Don't try to memorize long affirmations or phrases. Just get one or two key words which change the entire meaning. The most important thing here is to listen to yourself and notice what you are saying in your internal dialogues.

✧ *Use your intuitive "alarm system."* It tells you whenever you put thought energy into something that you don't really want. Remember, your Higher Self gives you a strong physical message, a "gut reaction." Request that your Higher Self or your guides establish some sort of dependable thought disruption. Adapting to your level of connection to their guidance, this can range from a sneeze to actual voices in your head saying "Hey! Don't think about that! Think about *this!*" As you get more connected to your guides, you may find they use a variety of methods with you.

Remember, it's *very* important to interrupt the thought pattern *at the moment it occurs.* Be deliberately conscious and alert. The best use of your mind comes from focused intent which requires staying in the moment. Negative thoughts are often what come to mind when you think back to old failures or look forward with fear at potential consequences. Without ignoring data from past experiences, use your imagination to visualize *all* possible outcomes–not just the negative ones! Balance the negative with positive thoughts. Do not take this as a suggestion to ignore a negative. Negative thoughts help you locate the fear; negative thoughts bring messages too!

Guilt and Shame

These two emotions create a form of self-abuse, your own energy turning back on itself. When you look at your actions (or your very being) with a harsh and judgmental eye, you bruise and weaken your inner spirit. Remember that your personal energy flows in a vigorous, constant stream. You literally inflict a forceful blow on that energy flow every time you cast a negative verdict against yourself. In this section, we define guilt and shame to insure clarity, and outline some practical paths back to JOY.

Guilt is triggered by your behavior; it is a negative emotional response to an action you took or some action you did not take. For example, feeling guilty about a hurtful thing you said to your spouse; feeling guilty because you did not repay a loan to a relative on time. In either case, the focus is not so much on the inner you, but on your behavior. Guilt has two varieties: *helpful guilt and destructive guilt.*

Helpful Guilt. If you have judged yourself by reasonable standards, it is likely that you experience little pinpricks of helpful guilt; this is a gentle form of remorse which helps you improve your behavior choices in the future. Helpful guilt is a trigger that promotes change. It works like a delicate alarm system to alert you to minor course adjustments necessary to stay on target to your goal. Helpful guilt creates an inner awareness that allows you to notice the choices that pull you off the most direct, joyful pathway. As you discover that some particular action (or non-action) causes a sensation that feels *less joyful,* the thing to do is identify the source of the sensation and make a correction. You may immediately amend the situation by apologizing or changing your behavior. In any case, replay the events in your mind, seeking to locate the moment of choice that took you off your path. Visualize another course of action that you feel would have lead to a more harmonic conclusion. Memory of the more appropriate behavior is now waiting in your memory bank, ready to generalize to the next similar situation. You may be surprised by the power of this technique. With helpful guilt, all traces of negative feelings disappear when you make the course correction. It does not linger unless you ignore it. If you persistently disregard "soft" helpful guilt, however, it becomes "hard" destructive guilt over time.

Destructive guilt is painful and intense, but it affects behavior change much less. For whatever reason, some of you have grown accustomed to the sensation of guilt, so you ignore whatever message it might have for you. At that point, you began to inflict guilt on yourself about almost *everything*—even things outside your range of control or responsibility. When you are feeling destructive guilt, you spend lots of time and energy trying to make amends for things you cannot change or correct, while ignoring your true areas of power. Such distortions in perception are common in disrupted energy systems, as if all the inner alarms are overloaded and go on and off at random. The guilt signals then become meaningless, and discovery of the source of the signal is much more difficult. People who spend lots of energy on guilt are invariably working with the destructive form.

The pathway out of destructive guilt needs to be traveled slowly and gently. To begin with, take little, low-intensity issues which cause you to feel guilty. Save the larger, more intense ones for later. Evaluate a particular event that invoked guilty feelings, looking for items that are outside your control. Your biggest block is a lack of self-honesty, commonly called denial. If, after thinking it through, you are unsure whether or not this is an issue involving helpful guilt or destructive guilt, gather more information. Use books, counselors, even friends to help you get a picture of where a harmonic and balanced boundary should be, but use your own intuition with regard to the information you get. It's *very* easy to lean too much on the opinions of others, for even a professional counselor can have a skewed perception of your issue. This "reality check" provides a model for comparison, however, a way to measure with a healthy yardstick. You'll likely discover some unrealistic belief at the core of your destructive guilt. For example, a mother who feels guilty whenever she says "no" to one of her children may have the unrealistic belief that she must make her children happy at all times. She's created a job description for herself that is impossible to carry out. She can correct this by focusing on the more realistic goal of teaching the children needed lessons in self-control and moderation, giving them skills to create their *own* happiness.

Shame is very different from guilt. It focuses on who you are, rather than your behavior. Shame is never helpful; it is always destructive and negative. It is the greatest hardship you can inflict on yourself, for it is about who you are, not what you do. Shame is the detrimental label you attach to yourself, such as "poor reader," "bad at math," "not good at sports." Once you accept the shameful label, you actually become that in your own mind, paralyzed and helpless to change. People very often feel shame over things they cannot control or change: physical appearance, ethnic background, intelligence level, the actions of relatives or friends to name a few. Some people feel shame over things which define only one aspect of who they are, such as their current financial status, their clothing, their automobile, or their weight. Shame is very damaging. With it, you paint your entire being with the same dull gray of personal humiliation, covering up the bright, beautiful colors of your soul, all of your positive traits and talents. Shame is the doorway to perpetual victimhood.

Eliminating shame is much like the cleaning of the wonderful paintings in the Sistine Chapel . . . once the grime of hundreds of years was gently and carefully removed, the art took on a completely new life and vitality. The original colors were much more vibrant than the art historians and art scholars ever imagined. All that had been written about Michelangelo's work had to be reevaluated in a new light. If you seek to eliminate the layers of shame that block out your own bright colors, remember to be kind to yourself. Use the same techniques suggested earlier for reducing destructive guilt. You must carefully research each part of yourself that you judge as unworthy, looking for unrealistic beliefs and perceptions. Go slowly and gently. You will discover positive qualities underneath what you believe to be negative. Remember, *there is nothing at the base of shame but fear, hiding the joyful choice of self-love.*

As you begin to make changes, your system recalibrates your internal belief structures. Whenever you change a single core belief, it triggers a domino-effect of changes to other beliefs that had been stacked together because of inferred connections. For this reason, a little work on shame often has significant effect over time. Move forward gently and slowly, secure in the knowledge that your focus on growth with joy will bring about efficient but pleasant growth. There is no need to be hard on yourself.

Chapter Ten

Pretty Poisons

Pretty poisons are situations and relationships that are appealing and attractive, but which pollute your happiness. It is an important life skill to be able to recognize these, just as it was vital for your ancestors to be able to recognize poisonous animals and tell toxic plants from edible ones.

In order to draw you in, pretty poisons use powerful magnetic attractors to capture and hold your attention. As you are moving through your life in a joyful manner, looking for those people and situations that are pleasing, you might easily be drawn toward a pretty poison. The deceptive quality works a lot like the "snapping" flower that eats insects; insects are drawn to the color and scent of the plant, which snaps closed around them only *after* they enter the heart of the flower. The insect must enter the plant, for the plant cannot chase and capture the insect. Our goal is to help you develop the skill to recognize pretty poisons very early on, eliminating the chance that you will enter the heart of a snapping plant!

Qualities of a Pretty Poison

✧ *Highly attractive on first contact.* These people and situations are almost "too perfect" to be true. This can be confusing, because people using growth with joy often create "too perfect" lifeplans for themselves. You can certainly protect yourself by eliminating all the attractive and magnetic situations from your life, but you must use growth with pain to do that! Instead, *take time* to check out every attractive situation, to observe and judge potential long-term consequences. Often the best people and situations grow on you over time. Pretty poisons are immediately attractive, but they soon develop cracks in the deceptive outer appearance.

✧ *Feeds your ego, not your soul.* When sincere compliments turn to flattery, you have entered a pretty poison zone. Your ego can be entrapped by any person, thing or situation that makes you feel more attractive, stronger or more powerful *without* roots in sincerity. You effectively (and sometimes literally) become addicted to this ego-builder. It happens with alcohol, cocaine, romances, even jobs. Try to be honest enough with yourself to realize when your ego is being fed, because at some point there will be a price to pay for that ego-meal.

✧ *Takes away real power, replacing it with false power.* Once you enter the pretty poison zone, you almost always lose your ability to see all possible choices. This is how your power shuts down, since your true strength develops as you make decisions and choices. The goal of the pretty poison is to keep you occupied until you get far enough into the situation to be "eaten." Often, you may not recognize your loss of power until—SNAP! When the consequences are revealed, it's too late. Your attention (and therefore your energy) had been misdirected into false power areas that mask your options.

✧ *Promotes pleasure not flow.* The flow state requires challenge and interaction, while pleasure is usually more passive. Self-esteem and personal power are elevated after engaging in flow activities, while both are reduced after a pleasure-oriented activity. Television can become a pretty poison, unless you work to transform TV-watching into a more active pastime (which is not an easy task). In relationships or work, watch for a lack of challenge because without it, the situation may shift into a pretty poison that eats away at your happiness.

✧ *Makes you fearful of losing or not having enough of it.* Many, many things can be either joyful or toxic, depending on how you handle them. Something becomes a pretty poison when you fear losing it. Things like wealth, fame and power commonly turn toxic, but are not inherently that way. Of course, objects of personal ownership are often in this category: houses, cars, jewelry, furs. When you work yourself to exhaustion to earn enough money to keep your "stuff," the beautiful things have become venomous to you.

✧ *Thrives on confusion rather than harmony.* In general, the chaotic atmosphere around a pretty poison is the easiest way to detect it. This confusion is the primary source of misdirection and deception. Please understand that toxic people or relationships are not usually deceiving you alone; they are almost always deceiving themselves most of all. People seldom acknowledge their selfish, ego-motivated actions for what they are; they create different, more palatable reasons for doing what they want. Confusion comes about when words do not match actions, or when actions do not fit a predictable range of behavior, but fluctuate wildly over time. Chaos allows hidden issues and plans to stay out of sight. Move slowly through chaos, retreating quickly if you cannot find any harmony and balance to use as seeds to grow more of the same.

✧ *Takes you further from yourself and Universal Truth; deeper into illusion.* Pretty poisons compel you to recreate yourself in someone else's image, rather than encouraging you to live your true essence more fully. Often, the illusion you find yourself in is a stereotype—society's image, or a parent's image. In this way, many jobs, titles and degrees can become quite toxic. For instance, a person may make a radical transformation from the struggling student to a well-defined doctor image as soon as he/she graduates from medical school. The same is true for ministers, lawyers; almost every profession, in fact. A denial of self can occur, with Self replaced by the stereotype, no matter how poorly it fits. When others react to the stereotypic self, the false personality, this causes the true self to disappear even more. This particular pretty poison may manifest in large-scale ways such as racism or other divisions between groups of people with differing religious or political beliefs.

You can learn how to test and verify whether you are involved in a pretty poison. There is a cycle that pretty poisons move through—from the initial magnetic attraction to the moment the consequences become apparent. You may have already recognized as toxic some events or relationships in your life. Extract yourself as quickly as possible from the pretty poisons already in your life. The primary skill you need to protect yourself from a pretty poison is awareness—to recognize it before you get too far in! As you look through legends and fairy tales from most cultures and civilizations, you'll notice that many have this as their subject.

Snow White is an obvious example, with many illustrations of the pretty poison concept within a single story. The Wicked Step-Mother is beautiful, but in spite of her surface appearance, she is evil to the core. She is one of mythology's strongest metaphors, particularly when she offers the poisoned apple to poor Snow White. In the complete tale, Snow White is skeptical and cautious on a few occasions when the poison is offered. Of course, she finally succumbs. Just imagine how much simpler it would have been if the Prince had met up with Snow White by dropping by the house of the seven Dwarves for tea! Years of trouble came from her choice to take a bite of that poisoned apple!

The Trojan Horse provides another reference to a pretty poison. The choice to open the gates of the city (to bring in the mysterious, fascinating horse) was the downfall of the city. Such over-abundance of trust is something unknown to you in this day and age. It may seem almost ludicrous to your contemporary mind that this simple trick would work so well, but do not miss the meta-phoric point of the story by taking it too literally. Pretty poisons are often obvious to others, but not to the victim! This story clearly demonstrates how easily deceived you are in the presence of a pretty poison focused on you.

The Genie in the Bottle is another good example of pretty poisons at work. In fact, there are many stories from around the world that are variations on this theme: three magic wishes, the first two of which make things worse until the dupe uses the final wish to return to his/her original state. It may be less obvious how this connects to the concept of pretty poisons, but these tales focus on the destructiveness of a lack of balance. A good situation will often be transformed into a poisonous situation; this happens when a person insists on having *too much* of something. Again, notice how important *choice* is to these stories. Also, the wishing person always seems to rush with his/her wishes allowing the genie (or whoever fulfills the wishes) to "get" them on some technicality or exact wording. Through this feature, the stories demonstrate why you need to be deliberate, especially when a pretty poison is trying to rush you along!

These are only a few of many stories which help humans work at recognizing a pretty poison in time. You might find it interest-ing and helpful to go back to these "encoded" lessons, seeking out the metaphors and connecting them to your life of today. Many of you have not thought about these kinds of stories since you were children, but these tales hold deep lessons that you spent time absorbing when you were young. Now is the time to be awake, aware, conscious, and deliberate. You might want to look back, especially at your favorites.

Stages of Progression

What is the general progression of an interlude with a pretty poison? We will look at this, and along the way, we have suggestions and pointers for behavior that will break the progression before the negative phase hits. Please realize that you often do not know *for sure* that something is a pretty poison—unless you go in too deep! You can sniff around it all day, just as long as you do not go through the critical doorway that slams shut behind you. Your choice to enter is required. You can *never* be forced into a pretty poison. However, you might feel as if you were if you refused to acknowledge all your options. *Take time to look things over before you enter.* Once you get in too far with a pretty poison, you may have to move through most or all of the progression. It's like getting on a roller coaster: once it starts moving, you have to finish the ride.

Stage One. The Baited Hook. The only way a pretty poison can draw your attention is by using bait that you find attractive. You never see hooks baited with other stuff that doesn't attract you. You are drawn to things you hunger for—unless you tried it before and learned a lesson. One of the most amazing things about humans (to us) is how easy it is for you to dismiss earlier lessons and experiences. When this happens, you can find yourself attracted to the same bait over and over. Remember, the bait is something that fills an empty spot inside you. If you're lonely, a companion who is secretive and mysterious may be the bait on the hook. If you're broke, a get-rich-quick idea may come along. If you look carefully for the empty holes inside yourself, you might even be able to predict the general type of bait that would be most tempting.

Stage Two. The Dance. Once the bait has engaged your attention, the interesting part begins. Generally, a pretty poison will dance in a pattern mirroring your own. The point of this is to establish some kind of harmony or synchronization between you. For instance, when faced with a get-rich-quick scheme, the "hook" is to show you how others just like yourself have done so well in the same situation. As you ask questions and listen to answers, the dance is happening. The dance is still a safe stage, however, because you are still just sniffing around. The pretty poison must get you so busy dancing that you do not notice the boundary between this stage and the next (the Gotcha Stage!) Be aware that the hook will keep your attention at all costs. The worst possible scenario for the pretty poison is that you step away from the dance. Often, the dance focuses your attention *away* from particulars that would alert you to potential consequences. When you step away, you gain clarity and perspective. This is why you've often heard it's a good idea to "sleep on it" before making a decision. Be sure to take time to step back from the dance. For instance, spend some time apart, even if your new romantic partner resists it. Before making a commitment to purchase a product, ask about a way to try a small sample. Your goal is to create some space between you and the hook—just enough space to loosen the extra magnetism that comes from being so close to what will (seemingly) fill your empty spot.

Stage Three. Gotcha! Assume you danced right through the doorway into Stage Three. Sometimes the door clanks shut behind you, sounding rather like a jail door! At other times, there's a quiet "click" at your back, and a door you never noticed is closed. Things begin to change almost immediately once you enter Stage Three. For example, the sweet fiance who becomes controlling (maybe even abusive!) within weeks of the wedding. Many abusive men follow this pattern, acting nice until there is a strong tie which will keep the partner around. Many types of pretty poisons work in "addiction loops" where the three stages happen over and over. For an alcoholic, this stage can consist of black-outs, DWI arrests, job loss, or divorce but it starts back at Stage One tomorrow. In fact, non-drinking alcoholics must resist Stages One and Two every day, because the door for Stage Three slams when they start drinking. The most difficult part of interacting with a pretty poison, is figuring out how far in is safe.

If the situation is not a pretty poison, Stages One and Two look pretty much the same. Take time during the *Dance* phase of a situation to figure out which it will be in Stage Three—a pretty poison or just pretty.

Some pretty poisons can be exited fairly quickly, as soon as you become aware of the situation. The ones with the quietly closing door are of this type. The ones that clang shut like a jailhouse door are usually the type which require you to finish the ride. As far as extracting yourself, each situation is different, though an important principle holds for all situations: *you must create distance between you and the baited hook*, particularly in an addictive loop. Pretty poisons may use a shift into a distorted form of logic, hooking you again by offering an easy "out" which actually keeps you in, so be aware of this. You need not "tame the lion," just get out of the cage as quickly as possible. This is more true than ever with today's faster, stronger energy. Pretty poisons are working faster than ever, too. Pretty poisons consume your energy, giving you little in return; bypass them for positive lessons and growth with JOY.

Chapter Eleven

Efficiency:
The Basis for Achieving Dharma

Now we present an extremely important topic, something we spoke of earlier in the book without much elaboration. Please do not take this information lightly, even if you are tempted to do so. The critical concept is *efficiency,* which is the basis for dharmic growth. Dharma is gained by using inherent cosmic principles and methods. Dharma occurs when no extra energy is expended in order to overcome blocks or fears. Dharma is the most joyful experience possible. In your search for growth with joy, efficiency is the vehicle that carries you most quickly toward your goal.

What kind of efficiency do we mean? All kinds, because you expend energy in many different ways. Each expenditure of energy is an opportunity to gain a little "dab" of dharma; it happens whenever you manage to use a situation to move *with* Universal Energy rather than trying to resist the flow. Chaos and confusion often lead to wasted effort and energy, while efficient action has a harmonious feeling and flows smoothly. Efficiency must also be flexible and fluid, however, for rigidity can also lead to wasted effort (especially when it's time for a change!)

Efficient thought patterns create an efficient flow in small, daily activities. From there, the efficient flow generalizes to larger life patterns—dharmic relationships and career, ultimately leading to magnificent peak experiences of joyous existence. Get the details of your life flowing efficiently, and notice how all aspects of your existence fall into place!

Principles of Efficiency

✧ *Establish clear goals.* Make lists of things you need to do: grocery shopping, household repairs, errands, phone calls to make, letters to write, bills to pay. If there are time limitations such as a certain day or time before which something needs to be done, add this information to your list as well. Write lists of medium and long-term goals (like family or career). This is time well-spent, because the thought-energy used while making the list is sending out a signal to the Universe to help you accomplish each goal. Much more gets completed when you create a list. (Note: This is an excellent way to start teaching very young children how to think clearly, which eventually leads to clarity of thought in adulthood.)

✧ *Create a circle.* Look closely at your "To Do" list for tomorrow. Think about how to combine the various errands or activities in a fluid, circular way. Try to ignore your habitual way of doing these activities just to be sure you're not overlooking another route or method. Look for an efficient way to move from one task to another, perhaps by combining items on the list. While running errands or shopping, plan a circular route that eliminates backtracking. When you're planning your day, create a "circle" of sorts in the way you move from one activity to another. Start out "close to home" or with some fairly easy warm-up tasks, move a little further out into more involved activities, then go deep into your hardest tasks before circling back closer to home with some final work (like making tomorrow's To Do list!)

✧ *Use your intuition to find shortcuts.* Pay attention to little flashes of insight that guide you into more efficient choices or pathways. As noted above, open-minded flexibility allows you to make necessary adjustments as soon as they hit your awareness. At times, these little jolts of intuition may seem to be slightly off-target from your goal, but experiment with them until you develop trust in your own inner voices and "gut" reactions. Once you trust your intuition, you can more easily take advantage of shortcuts, such as avoidance of traffic snarls or a modified schedule that puts you at a store the first day of a big sale.

✧ *Watch for "overlaps."* Efficiency improves dramatically whenever you combine overlapping items. If you combine the To Do lists of two people, the potential for overlap is greatly increased. As more people are added, the possibility of overlap increases exponentially. However, the potential for chaos also increases exponentially. In a group setting, it may be an expenditure of time and effort to establish clear goals by making lists or stating plans aloud, but it carries a very large pay-off when overlaps are combined to save energy. Again, flexibility and structure are needed to make this happen—structure in the statement of your goal, flexibility as you adjust things to fit in with the plans of everyone in the group. A terrific example of overlap efficiency is the international mail system. Imagine the inefficiency of a system where each person had to find his/her own way to get a letter or a package to someone else. The cost in wasted time and energy alone would be exorbitant. Another everyday example of efficiency is the use of computers, with all the various choices one has for sharing information (like computer bulletin boards and networks), as well as opportunities to streamline personal productivity.

✧ *Believe things can happen easily.* A difficult habit to break is the thought pattern that says you must work hard and struggle to achieve success. We are not saying that you can sit and watch television all day while things on your list magically get done. We *are* saying that you can enjoy what you do each day. Look for pleasant, fun, joyful ways to complete your list. If you really dislike something on the list, evaluate it closely, for it is a block to your efficiency. Perhaps it can be ignored or eliminated; maybe you need to develop more skill or knowledge about it. Now, look closely at your favorite activities on the list. Remember, dharma comes about when you achieve your goals while performing your most desired activities. You are uniquely skilled to complete whatever actions are needed for your dharmic joy! It could not be dharma unless it perfectly matched your abilities and desires; dharma occurs when you do what you do best with love and joy! Also, remember that the movement toward a goal is where the dharmic energy occurs, not from the sensation of reaching a goal. Pure joy comes from the climbing, rather than the view from the top of the mountain.

✧ *Review your goals; mark off the completed ones.* You complete a circle by taking this final action. Don't worry if everything on your list isn't completed. Mark off the tasks that are done, and move the rest to the top of a new list. This act provides a perception of movement, improving your sense of empowerment and demonstrating to you that you are making things happen. To Do lists of regular activities may stay current for only a day or two, but weekly, monthly or yearly lists are also useful. When you review a list to mark off completed items, you clear your mind for the future and the new list. Using lists has two other distinct functions: you reduce the chance that anything will get left out or lost; and you'll often work harder to get something done just because you're tired of writing it over and over on your lists!

You may wonder how efficiency in your grocery shopping and errands helps you achieve spiritual growth. The large patterns of your life are formed out of the small, intricate designs of your daily activities. If you are efficient in the small details, it is more likely that you will develop efficiency in the overall activities that fulfill your lifeplan. People who try to establish harmony and joy in their lives by quick, massive changes (a move across the country, a new mate, a new job) usually find that this method fails because the small, daily changes never happen. Over time, such people tend to find themselves scaling the wall of the same old circumstances, built over time by the same bricklayer (themselves) using the same old bricks (daily actions).

Likewise, abrupt, sweeping changes in your daily actions evoke more resistance than if you chose a gentler approach. Ease into the behaviors of efficiency, allowing yourself time to adjust and grow comfortable with each new habit. Changing thought patterns is a more complex activity than you might assume; a change in a single basic belief triggers many, many adjustments to connected beliefs and thought patterns. It takes time. Our recommendation is this: try at least one of our efficiency activities each day—make one list, create a "circle" route for running errands, review yesterday's list. Let these new habits of efficiency develop with dharma, easily and joyfully. As the new behaviors work for you, making your day flow more effectively with less effort, you will naturally be drawn back to them, repeating them again and again.

Section Three

Working with Energy

Chapter Twelve

Your Personal Energy System

Part A – Energy Basics

As lightworkers, you need to understand and use energy. This section of the book provides information on the manipulation of energy. Do not be fooled by the simplicity of our energy techniques; efficiency is often very simple. Even if you already know a great deal about energy, return with us to the basics. If energy work is new to you, be assured that this information makes it easy and safe.

Your energy is the non-physical representation of what you are feeling and experiencing. You can observe your energy to understand what is going on in your life, and you can manipulate your energy to *change* what you are experiencing. First, we explain how energy moves through your body. Then we offer some simple techniques for adjusting or controlling the flow of that energy. Current changes in the planetary energy affect your energy flow, intensifying the need for you to consciously manipulate your energy.

Describing the Energy System

Energy flows through your body with a predictable circulatory pattern, similar to the blood in your veins. There are "control valves" located all over your body; these are called *chakras*. You may be familiar with the seven most significant chakras which extend from the tailbone to the top of the head. These central chakras process the primary energy input, and regulate very large quantities of energy. In some teachings, the chakras are represented as spinning circles of energy, each corresponding to a particular color. Your aura contains layers of energy from each chakra, the seven colors blending and separating according to your energy flow. Each chakra is used for a certain type of energy:

- ✧ First chakra: survival of the body, self-protection
- ✧ Second chakra: sex and reproduction, creativity
- ✧ Third chakra: power, taking independent action
- ✧ Fourth chakra: giving love, receiving love (self-love, too)
- ✧ Fifth chakra: communication, expression
- ✧ Sixth chakra: seeing the energy aspects of the world around you
- ✧ Seventh chakra: sending intentions, receiving insight, soul awareness

In addition to the seven primary chakras, there are secondary and tertiary chakras which handle smaller volumes of energy flow to various parts of the body: particular organs, and to the arms and legs. If you want to learn more about the basic chakra system, there are numerous books and charts readily available to you.

For thousands of years, many methods for manipulating energy have been developed. Planetary energy is so fast and strong at this time, that even subtle energy movements are easily sensed and controlled with simple techniques. All that is required to adjust energy flow is a visual image of what you want to accomplish. Energy has movement qualities similar to a thick, sticky liquid, like honey. It is also golden like honey, but more "sparkly." Visualize the "honey/energy" flowing into whatever part of your body you choose, while you open the appropriate chakra(s). If you sense a resistance to the energy's movement, you have likely discovered a closed or blocked chakra. Visualize the chakra with a knob much like a faucet or volume control knob on a radio or television. In your mind, set the knob to adjust the flow to whatever setting feels right. Many people assume that more is better, but this is not so with energy. For some types of energy work, a very small flow is needed. In fact, too much energy can create as much difficulty as too little! Experiment to find a setting that feels comfortable.

What is a Chakra Blockage?

A chakra may be blocked for many reasons. There are different kinds of blockages, and various treatments for them. You can have a "jammed" chakra, with the knob "rusted" solidly into a particular position. This blockage happens when external circumstances make it feel unsafe for the energy of a particular chakra to flow freely. Over the years, you may develop a deeply-ingrained habit of holding that chakra at a particular setting. The chakra may be completely closed or partially open, but seldom is a chakra jammed in the full open position. As you visualize the "jammed" chakra, gently try to turn the flow control knob. If there is a feeling of resistance when you do this, *do NOT force it.* Remember, your goal is growth with JOY, a gentle and delicate way of dealing with things. Mentally apply oil to the knob, then leave it alone for a couple of days. During that time, you may find yourself processing some strong lessons; safely releasing some old emotions, feelings long buried within your body and energy system. It may take several applications of "astral oil" to open a badly rusted knob. The oil metaphor tells the Universe that you wish to gently open the valve. That image triggers whatever events or feelings are needed for you to experience a pleasant, harmonic opening of the jammed chakra. It may take some time. Do not rush this process.

Another way a chakra closes down is through a chakra spasm. Unlike the previous type of blockage, a spasm occurs in a chakra that is usually open. Certain events or situations trigger a sudden, sharp closure of the chakra. This type of blockage usually opens itself back up over time, sometimes in hours, perhaps in days or weeks. For some, the reopening may take up to a few months! When you experience a chakra spasm, you often develop a physical discomfort in the area of the closed chakra. When blocked energy collects and "ferments," this pool of stale energy is the source of your physical discomfort. If the blockage remains for very long, other physical symptoms may appear in adjacent areas, lower than the closure. For example, if the fifth chakra (throat) spasms, you may develop a sore throat or lose your voice. If the spasm continues, over time the problem may effect the area of the fourth chakra (heart) and manifest as a deep cough or pneumonia. Later in this chapter, we explain other ways your energy system becomes clogged, and more on how to "clean out the pipes." We also suggest additional energy exercises and practical applications.

Child and Adult Energy Systems

The energy system of a child is a bit different than that of an adult. The information provided here will help you to understand how the energy flow influences your child. Energy work with children can have very positive results, although most children in the pre-puberty stage have wonderful intuitive abilities to diffuse their own energy blockages. Understanding the energy system of children is also useful for adults as they work with their own energy, since certain energy blockages or problems often have their roots in childhood.

Please recall that the chakra system operates as a circulatory system for the energy in your body. The seven primary chakras work like valves to control the flow of energy in the system. Infants are born with their chakras at the "original factory setting," which is about 50 percent open. This is why children are, in general, easily influenced and controlled by adults (third chakra activity). This is also why very young children normally have less interest in sexuality (second chakra) than adults.

No matter what their age, people have different energy capacities—some large and some small. In your visualizations, energy systems may appear like different sizes of pipe passing through the primary chakras. One person might have a "pipe" the size of a garden hose, while another's resembles a large fireman's hose. By the way, each of you chose the size of your personal energy pipeline for this incarnation. Large or small, it fits with your lifeplan. Children with naturally large energy systems may have more "juice" at only 50 percent open, than an adult with a small capacity system which is completely open. An energy-strong child often dominates the unsuspecting adult! He/she needs leadership training from an early age, in order to develop sufficient skill and ability to manage the quantity of energy.

All children need to be taught about appropriate personal boundaries and personal power before puberty, for puberty is when the chakras begin to open to their full capacity. As the second chakra opens, physical changes and sexual awareness develops. As the third chakra opens, personal power increases and the youngster wants to make his/her own choices and decisions. (This is when it seems like open warfare in the household!) As the fourth chakra opens, the first case of "puppy love" hits the child like an arrow to the heart. As the fifth chakra opens, the child begins to desire intense communication with his/her peers. Usually, the sixth and seventh chakras do not open more than 50 percent until later in one's life, typically between 30 and 40 years of age. Very few people manage to get the first five chakras completely open before then! The higher chakras do not open fully because only a minimal flow is getting through to them.

What keeps the first five chakras from opening fully? Energy blockages are caused by unexpressed negative emotions, old, stale energy "stuffed" somewhere in the energy system. Some blockages form in early childhood, reducing the energy flow to *less* than 50 percent. The intensified emotions and new situations in the teen and early adult years often lead to energy closures and blockages of all kinds. The first broken heart, major blows to the power/self-esteem area, disappointment at unfulfilled expectations—all of these are triggers that can close off some section of a recently-opened chakra system. Reactions to such events demonstrate how well the young person is handling the new energy. At best, he/she expresses the negative emotions in a healthy manner, and then moves on to new experiences. Positive emotions are very intense as well. For this reason, mood swings and "high drama" are common to young adults. Healthy outlets for these high emotions are very important, because long-term problems develop when energy (whether positive or negative) does not flow out of the energy system.

Early childhood traumas like physical or sexual abuse cause a wide variety of energy disruptions that show up with more intensity when the system expands at puberty. Sexual abuse prematurely opens the second chakra beyond 50 percent, often resulting in sexual acting-out in the teen years. In adulthood, the sexually abused person must correct damage in order to get the second chakra comfortably open and flowing without spasms. Physical abuse often closes down the third chakra. When a person is threatened not to tell about abuse, this closes down the fifth chakra. Physical and/or emotional pain closes down the fourth chakra, the feeling center.

One of the most natural forms of self-diffusion children use to unblock themselves is play. Children express feelings with toys, art, movement, or music, helping the energy to move out of their bodies. It moves through the arm and hand (coloring or drawing), the throat (talking or singing) or the lower body (dancing or twirling). Most young children have a wonderful, intuitive ability to diffuse energy blockages. During the teen years, however, the energy system is harder to handle. When the energy flow suddenly increases, the discomfort of a blockage is much more intense. Still, the same expressive techniques for diffusion may be used.

In adults, if the sixth and seventh chakras open beyond 50 percent, there is improved psychic and intuitive abilities. Creativity and comprehension dramatically increases. Visual and intellectual areas are both enhanced. Not everyone wants to open these chakras to the maximum setting, however, for there is so much "out there" that pours in when these are wide open. If you experience unwanted psychic interludes (receiving too much information or sensation about the people around you), you might have unknowingly opened these chakras more than is helpful. Simply visualize the corresponding knob turning, gently closing until you reach a comfortable setting. Many psychics have a sense of "tuning in" and "tuning out" to the constant stream of psychic information that flows in the energy field around you at all times. Don't be afraid of being overwhelmed by rushes of energy; realize that you control the settings. It is as simple as turning a volume knob in your mind.

More Energy Basics

A tenet of acupuncture (as well as many other energy work techniques) is that pain occurs when energy flow is blocked. The acupuncture needle creates an alternate "exit route" for the energy to flow out of the blocked area, eliminating the pain. When you work on a blockage in some part of your system, take time to handle it gently. Energy builds up at a blocked area (or just behind the blockage), usually causing pain and discomfort that intensifies as the energy gets "stale." You can reduce or stop the pain by draining the excess build-up of stale energy and rinsing the area with clean, sparkly energy. Using the closest chakra *below* the blockage, imagine energy rinsing and draining out of the system. You can diffuse yourself with techniques that small children do naturally. Use drawing or writing through the fourth chakra. This helps fifth chakra blockages, draining from below. For a third chakra blockage, which you drain out through the second chakra, you can use sexual activity, walking, biking, dancing, even soaking your feet or lower body in water. With any of the above activities, just visualize the desired energy movement as you engage in the action. (More on unblocking chakras in the next chapter.)

If you are unsure if/where you have energy blockages, you can develop the ability to observe your own (or someone else's) energy system through simple internal visualization. Verbally, or in your mind, state your intention to see a particular energy system. Next, imagine a medical chart that shows a human figure with slightly outstretched arms. Visualize the "pipeline" that runs from the tailbone to the top of the head. At each of the seven chakras points, see a knob with numbers on it that tell you the flow setting of the chakra. If you are looking at secondary chakras too, you will see another series of smaller "pipelines" that run out from each major chakra, particularly into the legs (second chakra) and the arms (fourth chakra). You can observe any energy system once you create the visual "template" of this image in your mind. Whenever you need information about an energy system or a blockage, just take an "X-ray" look with your mind's eye.

Your goal is not necessarily to have your energy system fully open at all times. Explore what your own best settings are for different situations and activities. As you develop more awareness of how your energy moves and flows, you naturally increase your skill at deliberately widening or narrowing the chakra openings for whatever task is at hand. A masseuse for instance, focuses maximum energy flow through his/her hands during a massage, while occasionally using the sixth chakra (Third Eye) to observe the client's energy system and how it reacts to the energy manipulations. As another example, some athletes abstain from sexual activity before a big game or important athletic performance. This is a rudimentary way of building up energy in the legs, which is often crucial to sports activities. Sexual restriction is unnecessary, however, for someone who understands how to shift and focus personal energy into the desired chakra area.

As you develop more understanding of how your personal energy system operates from day to day, you readily notice disruptions that, if left alone, may trigger physical pain or illness over time. If some kind of blockage occurs, you can visually direct your energy to give your body a message that you want a harmonic energy flow. You may find that certain events or people trigger your energy system in certain predictable ways; over the long-term, this is what leads to major illness. Observation of the problem or imbalance is the doorway to its elimination. Look at your energy system, do some diffusion work, then check the system again to see what changed. Work of this kind provides you with a sense of control and skill which leads you to feel strong and empowered.

Breathing and Energy

Breathing influences your energy system. Use of breathing techniques can enhance energy manipulation a great deal. There are a variety of breathing methods, but they are difficult to describe precisely in words. Therefore, you may find it helpful to seek some training in breath work, such as that taught in yoga and in some forms of meditation, for example.

Your energy circulates both through and around your physical form, similar to the way your blood circulates in your veins and arteries. Your heart pumps blood; your breath pumps energy. In a sense, you breathe in your own soul, or essence, with each breath, for your body is simply an empty shell without your soul. Your breathing animates your physical form with your spirit, or non-physical consciousness.

As you may recall, the energy system of a child usually functions at 50 percent capacity, the "original factory setting," so to speak. In children, breathing is more frequent and rapid. The increased frequency of breath replenishes their systems more often. This is necessary because the volume capacity of their small lungs is not as large as adult lungs; unlike blood, however, the soul energy is not reduced for a child. The "volume" of your soul remains static over your entire lifetime. Less capacity in the system (or chakra pipeline) requires more frequency of breath needed to pump in enough "self" to properly animate the body.

Breathing difficulties in children are often indicative of trouble in anchoring the soul into the body. For instance, "crib death" (SIDS) is now recognized as a cessation of breathing while the infant sleeps. If the soul doesn't flow into the tiny body of an infant through strong breathing, the consciousness may not get securely "fastened" to that body. Sometimes, crib death is like a hotel reservation "no-show." A soul makes plans to enter the body shortly after birth, but makes last minute changes. If another soul doesn't immediately show up to take the "reservation" for the body, there will not be enough breath to sustain it.

Humans sleep to fully recharge the physical system. The most important component of sleep is the hours of deep, slow breathing that occurs. Think of how terrible you feel when you have trouble breathing at night, and how tired and cranky you feel the next day. "Not quite yourself" is more true than you realize, since you have not completely filled up your body with your essence during the night. As you might guess, that is why children require more sleep than adults. The extra hours of deep breathing are needed to fill their bodies through the reduced capacity of their energy system. More hours at less volume per hour gets the job done.

Sleep disorders often indicate some difficulties with the flow of air (and soul energy) into a physical form. REM sleep comes when you have filled the energy system enough to feel oneness with your Higher Self. You often bring back recollections of these encounters as dreams. As you may imagine, connecting with your complete essence from time to time is needed for balance and sanity. Please remember that sleep revitalizes your consciousness, not just your body. If sleeping difficulties or your schedule make it hard for you to get plenty of sleep, a few breathing breaks through the day will help you feel better. It is interesting to note that some yogis require very little sleep because of their consistently deep, strong breathing.

An interesting oddity to breath energy is the yawn. This deep, involuntary breath occurs when your system is running low, when you need some more of "yourself." If you practice appropriate breath work all day, yawning will not occur. If you find that you yawn often, you may need to work on improving your breathing techniques. A sigh is another signal that you need extra energy, usually in the heart chakra area. A sigh pulls more air into the lungs while a yawn pulls air down into the diaphragm. Often, a sigh comes when you are sad or depressed, emotionally drained in your heart chakra. Visualizing an energy flow to the area will help.

Following are some pointers on how to improve your breathing. These techniques will probably require much of your attention for a few days (or even a couple of weeks) before old habits change. Even as you work on making these adjustments permanent, however, these methods are effective as "band-aids," to be used as needed until you develop better and consistent breathing habits.

✧ *S. . L . . O . . W . . L . . Y!* The minimum breathing time should be about six seconds, three seconds in and three seconds out. Over time, try working up to about ten seconds. Then, keep going and see if you can get to fifteen seconds! (Tip: To extend the length of your breath, breathe in... hold... breathe out... hold.) Counting each step of the breath will help you concentrate your thoughts on your breathing. This may seem extraordinarily hard at first, but such well-ingrained habits are hard to break. Practice anytime you are waiting for something or not otherwise mentally occupied—while driving, stuck in traffic, in line at the bank, in the shower or tub.

✧ *In through the nose, out through the mouth.* The main cause of general shallow breathing is in the exhale. If the lungs are not fully emptied, that much less new air can be brought in. Your throat provides a larger pathway than the nose and sinuses to empty the lungs. If you have not been exhaling sufficiently for a long time, the concentration to push out through the throat reminds your body to exhale completely. Some people have a tendency to hold onto energy once it enters their system (a habit often developed based on issues of abundance). This "hoarding" mentality, conscious or subconscious, just doesn't work! New, fresh energy is constantly required. You must steadily replenish your "old" supply of air-energy, keeping it fresh and vital, flowing like a river. Your supply is endless and infinite; stockpiling energy, air or any other form of energy, is seldom useful.

✧ *Visually send breath to all parts of your body.* Use your mind's eye to envision the internal effects of your breath work. "See" the air entering your body with each breath. As you inhale, the fresh new air is sent from the lungs to all other parts of your physical form, exchanged for "exhaust fumes" which are then expelled with the exhale. Be sure to visualize plenty of air going to your brain, as it requires tremendous quantity to operate well. If you have any physical difficulties, be sure to mentally send extra air to the affected parts of your body while *consciously ridding yourself of "exhaust fumes."* This method works to minimize discomfort, but only if you also eliminate build-up of old stale air-energy.

✧ *Use the diaphragm to breathe.* Using your diaphragm (just below your stomach—third chakra area) to breathe will help you use stronger, more powerful breaths, in and out. When you are breathing properly with your diaphragm, you will see more movement in your lower abdomen. When your breaths are shallow, the primary movement is in your chest. By using the deep breathing technique, you will increase your own personal power. In fact, the third chakra is where your power energy lies, so this is extremely important if you are working on leadership issues (which most of you are). Any time you feel the need for more personal power, several deep breaths from the diaphragm will energize your power center.

✧ *Understand your individual energy system.* Every energy system is distinctive, with subtle differences and idiosyncracies in how the energy flows. In order to compensate for these personal variances and blockages to your energy, you must study your own system. In a safe, quiet atmosphere, breathe consciously for five minutes or more. Explore yourself to observe what your energy is doing when the system is fully charged. Move your focus around your body to see what each individual part feels like. You may feel tension or tightness in some areas which may indicate some type of blockage or reduction of energy flow. Use guided imagery techniques to allow your Higher Self or your guide to visually "show" you what's going on in your system, as well as how to correct the problem. There are countless "glitches" that can occur in an energy system. This why there are countless techniques for energy healing, and almost all of them use strong, deep breathing to enhance their effectiveness. The more you know more about breathing, the more you can use it to facilitate a healing process.

✧ *Practice patiently.* At first, you may feel rather foolish or inept when trying out new breathing methods. Be gentle with yourself, for breathing is probably the strongest, most ingrained habit that you have. It is not easy to make quick changes in this area. Persistence is helpful. The rewards from this work are not instantaneous or easy to obtain, but they are life-changing in a subtle fashion.

Part B – Energy Blockages

Causes and Treatments

What is an energy blockage? What causes it, and what gently removes it? One kind of block, Type X, is caused by a closed or almost-closed chakra. This is what we previously referred to as a "jammed" chakra. A Type Y blockage, previously called a chakra spasm, is caused by an obstruction in the energy pipeline. It blocks energy flow much like a knot of grease and hair clogs up your kitchen drain. This is a "ball of fear," usually caused by some physical and/or emotional trauma. Victims of abuse often have hard rocks of negative energy blocking certain areas of their energy system. The most common block is Type Z, which has not been mentioned before now. With this type of blockage, the flow is diminished rather than completely blocked, by a residual build-up inside the pipeline. The "fear energy" is distributed over a wider area, and for this reason, can be more difficult to detect.

Your internal energy enters your body at the base of your spine (first chakra), moving upward through the other chakras. Like your blood, it flows out into your extremities through "secondary" chakras, often called "pressure points" or "acupuncture points." You can have a blockage anywhere in the internal system. If you have a particular physical ailment, use its position to help you locate the block. The problem area will be at the exact spot of the blockage, or where the energy "backs up" just inside the block. For instance, a blockage at your third, or Power, chakra, might cause flu symptoms in the stomach or the intestinal tract between the third chakra and the second chakra. Either symptom would pinpoint the block as being in or near the third chakra.

An important skill for working with energy is the ability to gently remove energy blockages. Energy flows within your internal system (in and around your physical body) as well as in a mutual transfer between people. The closeness of your relationship with another person determines the amount of energy that flows between you, and the balance of that energy exchange determines the harmony of the relationship. You can use visualization to remove blocks from internal and external energy patterns.

Each chakra has a particular application in external energy exchanges. Some chakras only send, some only receive, and some do both. It is possible to send and receive from chakras one, two, four, five and seven, but four is the strongest. The third chakra (Power) is only able to send energy, so it is not available to use for external energy transfers. The sixth chakra is only able to receive energy, collecting it through the Third Eye. The strongest chakra for external energy exchange is the fourth (or Heart) chakra, as this is the central chakra of your system. Some people may use only their second (or Sexual) chakra for energy exchange, common among people who have an addiction to sexual activity. Sex becomes their only way to energetically interact with other people, with the second chakra as the only available outlet for them to give and receive energy. This situation is commonly caused by a tremendous block at the third or fourth chakra.

External energy flow represents the movement of love between two people. For a good interaction, each person must have a moderate to strong flow at the fourth chakra, along with the capacity to both give and receive love. Blockages to these external valves are not always the same as blockages to the internal valves. It is possible to have good internal flow, but have a closed external valve or a blockage in the external "pipeline." The opposite is also possible. If you send love to someone who cannot receive it, your own energy can get "backed up" into the heart chakra area, maybe even as far back as the third chakra. This requires a "ground wire" to release the pressure. Imagine a wire of energy running from just before the block out to the ground. You need not quit sending out the love energy, for some day the other person's blockage may suddenly open up!

Use the same basic techniques to work on your energy blockages, both internal and external. Use your visualization skills to explore your energy system, locating any disruptions in the flow. Remember, the energy is like sparkly honey, flowing gently and slowly. Notice any spot with less sparkle; this is where negative energy pulls the sparkle out of your system. A completely dark area denotes a complete block of your energy flow. Diagnose the type of block, as described above. If completely closed, Type X can look just like Type Y. You may need to visualize the flow knob and turn it to see if anything happens. If only partially closed, Type X can look a lot like Type Z. Again, visualize opening the flow knob and see if an adjustment corrects the flow. Type Y can be the most difficult to eliminate, depending on how hardened the block has become over time. Picture the energy system, looking closely at the Type Y block. Imagine touching the block with a medical tool to test its hardness. Gently apply a sparkly "energy-lotion" to the blockage, softening it and preparing it to dissolve. This may require several applications. Use your intuition on frequency and timing, but most people need at least 48 hours between applications, sometimes longer. Type Z can also be hardened and needs the same gently-applied "energy-lotion." Once softened, both Y and Z should be rinsed with fresh energy. Be sure to picture the rinse-energy draining out of the entire system, perhaps through a hand. If not thoroughly rinsed, the negative energy can settle into some other area. You can place two fingers into a glass of water to receive the "dirty rinse water," then pour it down the drain with fresh tap water.

Energy Techniques

Here are some additional energy techniques that are useful for removing blockages and increasing energy flow. Each of these methods is fairly simple to put into personal use, and none of them require a professional facilitator. We advise that you experiment with each to discover which feel most comfortable and effective for your own energy system. Don't be fooled by the whimsical quality to some of these techniques; any time you work with metaphor and visualization, you are doing powerful energy work. You are simply communicating in a more Universal language than the spoken or written word.

 ✧ Method One: "Prayer Grease"

   When to use it. This technique is most effective for individuals feeling stuck or blocked at bringing in new things: new relationships, new jobs, new abundance of any kind, etc. Visually observe your personal energy system, either by seeing the aura directly or by a visualization (provided by your guides) of the internal chakra system. If you see "dark spots" where the sparkly energy flow does not travel, or if you notice a "pinched-in" section of the chakra system, this will be a good method to try. (*Note:* If you are completely blocked off at any point in your primary chakra system, this method will not be useful.)

How does it work? There are two components to this method. First, you must convert your desire or intention into a visual energy format. You transfer *anything* that you desire into a visualized ball of pure energy. For some people, it's no problem to mentally transform a thought into an energy ball. For others, more of a system is needed to complete the conversion. You can visualize your "prayer," your thought/energy ball, ascending a ladder that has larger squares at the bottom, which get smaller and more refined as you go higher. This "energy ladder" represents the degree of coarseness for the energy in the object. Thus, you are literally making your prayer or intention more compact and easier to transmit through a moderately-blocked system. The second part of the technique is to mentally add the "Prayer Grease" to your energy ball. This is a thin layer of very fine, very high-quality energy. Imagine it as liquid diamonds, burning almost like fire. After adding this to your intention (the energy ball), visualize your "greased prayer" moving through your chakra system—up through the Crown Chakra at the top of your head, shooting up into the sky above you like a shooting star!

Frequency. Use this method as often as you like. Of course, always be sure to be in a non-negative state of mind whenever you work with energy. This technique works fairly well if you are in a neutral state, but maximum effect comes from a positive energy state of mind.

Secret of its success. When you transform an intention into pure energy, you tend to leave out the areas of ambivalence you might unconsciously feel about really receiving what you are desiring. For instance, let's say you want to write and publish a book. Each time you energize that goal, you also energize some fears and negatives that immediately come to mind as soon as you think of the book. (If this were not true, you would already *have* this intention.) When you convert the book to an energy ball, the positives remain while the negatives are left out.

✧ Method Two: "Making Soup"

When to use it. Use this whenever you feel confused, faced with mysterious ingredients. If you find yourself confronted by people, situations and/or lessons that don't appear to fit together or make sense, this method helps you to move forward into comprehension and completion. You may feel besieged when a variety of issues come at you simultaneously. This results in a form of "soul overload," where you shut down on all lessons. It is more efficient to keep your growth moving along, so it is helpful to discover the various connections between your issues.

How does it work? Make a list of all the various components of issues that seem to be coming at you from all sides. Convert these issues into foods or seasonings. Be creative and have fun with this. There is no right or wrong way to do this. Allow your guides to drop ideas and insights into your mind. Some examples: You've been feeling cranky lately = crab meat. You've been angry at someone = cayenne or jalapeno pepper. You've been feeling small and vulnerable = baby shrimp. You've been afraid of something = chicken. Someone else is behaving unpredictably, a bit crazy = nuts. In your imagination, place all these ingredients into a large cooking pot. Add plenty of water (which represents your feelings about all these issues). Let these "ingredients" simmer on *very low heat* for a day or two. Then, go back into your visualization and taste your soup. If it does not taste good, add anything else that comes to mind. Then, simmer it again for another day or two. Continue this until the flavors meld and you enjoy the taste. See yourself eating up bowl after bowl of your delicious soup, which represents a willingness to absorb and process your current lessons and issues. On a practical level, this energy work pushes your lessons into an observable synchronization, allowing you to see the pattern. It also helps you "ingest" the issues comfortably.

Frequency. A single application is usually enough, but please realize that the results may be subtle and gentle. The single application might take up to a week to process, and a few more weeks to see or feel tangible progress. You can repeat this whenever you get a new menu of ingredients.

Secret of its success. The real magic of this method occurs at the naming of the metaphors. Often, you gain perspective on the true nature of the issue. Also, you often find the metaphors humorous; laughing as you work toward solutions is the most joyful way we know to create personal growth.

✧ Method Three: "Waiting at the Bus Station"

When to use it. It's easy to move into frustration and impatience while waiting for what you want. Timing can be very tricky. If the bus comes too soon, you may not be prepared for what it brings to you; if the bus takes too long, you may give up and leave the waiting area. If you are clear about what your intentions are, if your energy system is open and unblocked, and if you are just watching and waiting for things to arrive, this method is the one for you.

How does it work? Visualize a bustling bus station (or train station, or airport, or seaport—as you wish). Check on the arrival schedule for your particular intention (person, event or whatever). Go to the information desk, talk to the clerk there about your "whatever" —ask any questions you like about the arrival time, gate location, reason for delays, etc. This provides a way for your guides to offer you input in metaphor form about your current standing with your intentions. The clerk is actually one of your guides, answering your questions. Please realize that many layers of information lie in each reply. If you must wait, we suggest that you go explore the bus station—be sure you know where your arrival gate is, the baggage claim area, the bathrooms, etc. You may even like to talk with the workers who communicate with the bus drivers to update schedules and review maps and charts. This technique provides an active outlet for you to monitor progress of your plans and intentions, tracking them right to their arrival.

Frequency. Use as needed. You may need to update your information from time to time, particularly if your guides report weather or equipment problems with your bus. These represent short-term delays only. If things are temporarily fouled up, you will at least know about the delay *plus* you'll have a mechanism to find out when things get on track again.

Secret of its success. This entire metaphor helps you to understand the external complications that can tangle up a perfectly organized bus schedule/lifeplan. Remember that no matter what kind of delays might occur, the bus station has continual movement and flow, which is true of life as well. Instead of feeling isolated and blocked, frustrated and cranky, you can use this visualization to find your intentions amidst the rush and clutter of energy moving around the planet right now.

Part C – Energy in Objects and Places

Energy is Everywhere

Everything you see or sense is a form of energy. Energy flows through your body, and can be moved and manipulated through the chakra system. Energy also flows within every physical object on the planet. Actually, this energy originates outside the physical plane. It causes movements at the sub-atomic level that are the source of what you observe as physical reality. Everything—animal, plant, rock, drop of water—contains the same energy that moves through your own body. The sympathetic vibrations and interactions of all this energy is what living on the physical plane is all about.

You exist in an "energy soup," which you dove right into when you were born. Do you comprehend the mass of external energy influence all around you each day? Fully-sentient beings (including humans and cetaceans) have the highest potential to process energy on this planet. The actual manifestation of this potential varies greatly from soul to soul, particularly from younger souls to more experienced old souls. You came to this planet just to experience Earth's particular energy.

There is a wide variation of energy potential among animals, depending on their degree of consciousness. Size contributes to energy levels in animals also, but not every large animal has more energy available than every small animal. Suffice to say, this is a simple but complex system at work. Moving out of the animal world, consciousness shifts into a different gear for plants, minerals, structures, objects, and locations. American Indian and other spiritual doctrines teach about the thread of consciousness tying all things together . . . that thread is the energy that moves in and around all physical forms.

Now that the intensified energy is completely and fully operative on Earth, it's more common for everyone to notice and observe different energies. Realizing this early in the transformation is critical for members of your group, whether you are part of Wave One or late Wave Three. Your group plans to heal others by harmonizing energies wherever possible—through energized people, places and things! Each of you needs superbly-developed sensitivity to energy, and many of you need well-developed skills at manipulating energy.

Noticing Energy

Many of you will make amazing observations and discoveries simply by *noticing*. Your own energy sensitivities are expanding at the same time as the energies themselves have strengthened. This information may seem interesting and playful, but there is great value in the practice of energy observation. In the near future, new industries will sprout up based on these principles. For instance, the Orient has an ancient practice called Feng Shui, which is based upon harmonizing the energies of a location. Many businesses and careers will require such energy skills. Start practicing now, so you will be prepared as awareness expands gently into mainstream consciousness over the next five to ten years. Here are some areas to begin observing immediately:

1. *Food.* Restaurants and food stores of all kinds are very important because the energy from the food actually enters into your own energy system. People have long understood that the energy of the cook and the food-server enters the food. Why is a "home-cooked" meal considered a valuable item? Everyone recognizes the extra energy in food prepared by a loving cook. Pay attention to the energy of the people and the locations where you purchase food. If the cook and the waitress both hate their jobs, you may find the food doesn't settle into your system harmoniously. Remember, energies are more intense now, and food energy is much more noticeable.

2. *Objects.* Furniture, clothing, artwork, jewelry, plants and more, all have stronger energy pulses to observe. Surrounding yourself by objects that blend with your own energy is more important than ever before. Perhaps you have already noticed that new clothes have stronger energy than most old clothes. Think of the feeling of wearing something new for the first time. It energizes you for awhile, but the sensation usually

fades over time. There are ways to build stronger energy into your wardrobe, but first just observe the energies. On certain days you'll find it almost impossible to wear any color but the one that fills your aura. You may often find yourself wearing neutral shades, as this solves the problem of clashing wardrobe and aura energies. If you feel a strong desire to wear a particular color, you may *need* that color to balance your overall energy or to strengthen that spectrum for the day. Apparel color is not as trivial as you might think. Pay attention to the sensation you experience when you indulge your feelings; occasionally try to go opposite your feelings. Test the sensations. As you progress, you may want to experiment with objects such as furniture or jewelry. You can change their energy with visualization methods. *Note:* Wood is holding energy much stronger now than before the energy shift. Metals conduct energy quickly, but can be magnetized to a particular energy so that it seems to be holding it. (Actually, it is a constant flow of the same energy, similar to an electrical current.) Crystals and stones have *many* changes in their energy tendencies, variances of all types. If you've worked with them before, go back and test. You may get vastly different results because of the speed of new energy. You should not assume anything is the same.

3. *Places.* Structures have a complex energy, configured out of the individual energies of the raw materials mixed with the energies of the architect and construction workers. Then, the energies of the people who spend time inside the structure are layered on day after day. Extremely old buildings have complex and intricate energy systems much like a very old tree or an old person. How about an old church transformed into a disco . . . interesting energies mixed up there! Naturally, the most recent occupant energies are there on the surface like the most recent coat of paint on top of countless layers of wallpapers and paint. It is possible to clean out those cluttered old energies, scraping off layers until you get

down to the basic raw material energy. You can use a wide variety of methods, but a simple visualization (best done by a small group of like-minded people) will do the trick nicely. Before cleaning everything out in one swoop, however, why not spend a little time exploring the layers of energy? You can practice your energy-sensitivity skills, and you might find a really powerful harmonic layer worth keeping. Rather like finding a lovely mural by Michelangelo under some ugly wallpaper!

Ghost problems often come from heavily-embedded structure energies (which aren't a true ghost) or from a spirit which was magnetically drawn to the structure energies before it got to the astral doorway. This is why a haunting is usually attached to a home rather than the cemetery where the body was laid to rest. (Actually, cemeteries generally have relatively neutral energy levels, mostly grief balanced by calm gardeners' energy.) Start tuning into the energy of the places you go. Develop the skill to separate occupant energies on the surface from the deeper structure energies. *Tip:* Complex, hand-done work in the construction usually adds powerful energy, for most workers doing this type of work are in a flow state. You can notice the energy no matter where you go.

4. *Group Energy Fields.* A group energy field occurs whenever there are two or more people in the same space. (Side note: Telephones and computers create a "virtual" space that also creates a type of energy field, but it is more subtle and therefore much harder to discern than people sharing physical space.) Communication causes individual energies to blend, much like stirring ingredients together in the kitchen. Each of you has a fairly sophisticated sense of group energy, even if you never realized it.

First develop more conscious skill at perceiving group energies, then begin to explore how to use your personal energy to bring balance to the group field as a whole. There are many ways to do this:

* Change the "flavor" of your own energy (a strictly interior process that others may not even notice!)

* Change your physical location in the room.

* Ask a question on the topic that is unspoken but hanging in the energy field.

* Use one-on-one conversation to help another person shift his/her energy into a more harmonic blend with the whole.

There are countless other methods. Utilize every part of your day to experiment and observe your results.

One key to successful completion of your group lifeplan, described earlier as the White House group, is that all interactions *must* be harmonic. This means problems and differences require creative solutions that are positive for *all persons involved*. Since clear communication is not yet a common skill, it is *very* helpful if you can sense small disruptions within a group energy field. This allows you to be aware of a difficulty, like an early warning system, long before it causes bigger problems. Even if only a few humans on the planet are consciously bringing group energy fields into more harmony, there is a huge cumulative effect on the planetary energy field.

Chapter Thirteen

Using Your Energy

Part A – Power Auras

Working with Your Own Power Aura

The Power Aura is an isolation of third chakra energies, and it demonstrates the strength of your personal power. As you may recall, we first described the Power Aura in the second section, Chapter 8: Relationship Skills. There is a three-stage process in using the Power Aura for improving your relationships:

Observe

How do you use your Power Aura? Do you follow any patterns, such as Bully/Victim or Runner/Chaser? Be honest with yourself, use your intuition, then verify your behavior with observation. You generally use one pattern predominantly, but it's common to find that you use particular patterns only with certain people. At the most basic level, you are likely to find a predominance of one of these three behaviors:

1. Rigidly flat Power Aura, with occasional "explosions" when pushed too far.
2. Rigidly large Power Aura.
3. Flexible Power Aura, with fragile boundaries.

Decide

As you study your behavior in relation to your use of the Power Aura, determine what skills you have already, and where you may need improvement. There are five skill areas to consider:

1. Ability to expand Power Aura.

2. Ability to reduce Power Aura.

3. Ability to hold a firm boundary when others push at you.

4. Ability to hold a firm boundary when it leaves a gap between your Power Aura and that of another person.

5. Ability to monitor that your boundaries are appropriate.

No matter what pattern you have been using, you already have plenty of practice with at least one or two of these skills. If you have a rigidly small or large Power Aura, you know how to hold a firm boundary, but you need to learn about flexibility. If you move your boundaries in and out to match everyone you interact with, your lessons will be about how to hold firm boundaries. Everyone has a strength to build upon.

Visualize

The most wonderful thing about the Power Aura is the easy and gentle way it creates change. You need only create the *image* of your goal, and the Universe brings you whatever you need to achieve your objective. This *does not* mean that you have nothing at all to do, but it *does* mean that the necessary changes will happen in the most gentle and pleasant way possible. This is how you do it:

1. Convert a particular relationship into Power Auras. This allows you to view the relationship in its most basic energy configuration. Simply create a picture in your mind of yourself sitting with the other person. Include images of what you think the two Power Auras currently look like. If you cannot hold the auras in the pattern you want to *create*, allow them to take on the pattern that forms without your

conscious direction. Your Higher Self is giving you information, that's all.

2. Next, change the picture into what you desire to be the final outcome. Imagine the Power Auras gently and smoothly re-shaping themselves, expanding or shrinking fluidly. To represent your boundaries, include metallic gold borders on the Power Auras. If you want stronger boundaries, visualize them thicker. If you want more flexible boundaries, picture them moving like elastic; they stay strong, but expand and contract as you direct them. You need not reduce the thickness. In our view, the ideal auric pattern for any good relationship looks like this: Two Power Auras with strong flexible borders that meet in the middle, with an occasional "undulation" movement of about 10% of the thickness of a single aura. This movement demonstrates flexibility, meaning both people maintain closeness throughout the normal ups and downs of life. Rigid borders are not required.

3. Hold the idealized image for a few seconds. Enjoy the sensation. Visualize you and your partner smiling at each other. Now, change the vision into a snapshot that radiates golden light. Picture the snapshot floating up, and then down into the top of your head, sliding down until it settles near your heart at the fourth chakra. This insures that all changes to create this future will occur gently and lovingly. The metaphor establishes that you are creating these changes with energy from your heart. It also demonstrates that you hold this relationship near your heart.

4. Over time, a gentle awareness of small changes in your behavior occurs. This energy work may have some effect on your partner, but it instigates an extremely strong influence on your own thought and action patterns. Information and lessons come into your life, moving you gently toward the needed insight and skills.

Part B – Helping Others

The recent energy shifts are creating behavior changes in people who had not previously reacted to the new, more intense energies. For this reason, you can more easily discern whether someone has chosen growth with pain or growth with joy. Remember to maintain your own stance in neutral or joy; use all your skills to assist others when you can without slipping into negative energy yourself. *If you cannot assist without moving into negative, get out of the way to make room for someone else to help.*

Interestingly enough, people using growth with pain are becoming more polarized from people using growth with joy. This becomes readily apparent in your day to day activities and interactions with others. Please recall that up to now, many souls have been swinging back and forth from pain to joy—for some, many times within a single day. Energy intensification ultimately causes these shifting souls to land on one side of the "neutral fence" or the other.

You have many opportunities to observe what primary state the people around you have chosen. If two interacting souls operate from different polarities (joy versus pain, in this case), there is an increased probability for conflict, usually originating from the person choosing growth with pain. Be aware that the "pushing" that may come about, is caused by the meeting of two polarities. While this is a time when those of you in joy can choose to shift into negative, this street moves in both directions! This is also a time when those in negative can readjust and choose joy!

Transformation can occur in a twinkling! Do not assume that any person, no matter how negative they seem today, will remain in negative when tomorrow comes. Because of the speed and intensity of current planetary energies, anybody can make a dramatic and exciting metamorphosis, literally overnight! Changes that might have earlier required years of therapy or work in personal growth, can happen in just a few months! A shift in basic intent is all that is required.

What do you do if a negative person is "in your face?" How do you handle a confrontation with someone seeking to pull you into their whirlpool of growth with pain? Each situation has different, helpful responses to consider as possibilities: words, action, and silence at the appropriate time. There is one all-purpose response, however, and that is for you to create an intention to send a copious quantity of light energy to the negative person. Visualize this happening in your mind's eye. This action does not interfere with free choice, but it *will* help bring forward any hidden positive energy within the seemingly negative person. Sending light energy changes the balance of negative/positive; it either pulls the other person into closer energy alignment with your positive energy, easing the conflict, or it intensifies the polarity. If the latter occurs, the negative person is likely to pull away from that which is positive (you). Either way, the interaction changes for the better, providing more comfort for both parties.

Use this process with family, friends, co-workers, and even strangers (like store clerks, for instance). Send the light energy at the very moment you sense conflict or negativity, while you are still in physical proximity to the person. Actually, you can send light energy to someone when you are not physically near them, as well. You can send light energy as often as you like. It is non-invasive, for it is not "ingested" by those who have no desire to accept it. The light energy is never wasted, for any that is not absorbed will continue flowing until it finds someone who wants it! Use this simple technique as often as you like.

Extending a Helping Hand

One of the easiest ways you can be pulled into negative is by watching someone you care about suffer the consequences of choosing growth with pain. This inner reaction starts in your energy system, usually as a "mirroring" response to the negative energy in another person. Some stages of soul development have more tendency to mirror energy than others. You must observe yourself to discern how easily you slide into matching energy to the people with whom you spend time. It is *vital* that you learn how to disconnect your internal energies from overly-strong influences of those around you, particularly negative energies. This has been called "developing personal boundaries," or "completing a separation." Whatever name you use, you need to do it!

Does this mean that you should not care about what others are feeling, especially when they are in pain or discomfort? Of course not. However, *you cannot help someone get out of negative by getting in there with them.* If a person is dangling off a steep cliff, hanging on by their fingertips, you can help them much more from a stable, secured position. If you get beside them, hanging by your fingertips also, you only double the potential for catastrophe. Keep this visual image in your mind when faced with a friend or relative who is obviously on the "edge of the cliff." (We will continue to refer to the metaphor of someone hanging on the cliff, and this refers to any person who is in a negative energy crisis: depressed, distraught, anxious, highly upset, suicidal etc.)

How can you safely offer a helping hand? If you get into a negative state yourself, how can you ask for and receive a helping hand without putting another soul at risk? There are five important concepts to use to help another at this time, when personal energy is so erratic for many souls:

1. *Whatever you do, don't look down!* Just as you've seen in the movies, looking down from the edge of the cliff instills a sense of panic that increases the probability of falling. If you are feeling negative, it's time to look at where you are *at this moment.* A tremendous amount of pain comes from worrying; imagining all the worst-case scenarios with each image getting more negative than the last. When you are hanging off the cliff, look instead at your immediate surroundings.

Seek toeholds however tiny, to climb upward. If you are trying to help someone else, your job is to pull the negative person's attention upward to where you are; use questions and comments that shift his/her focus toward what the person *does want* instead of what he/she doesn't.

2. *Consider every possible option.* Negative persons may be rigidly holding tightly to a certain perspective, an angle that doesn't allow them to see all their choices and options. If you are the one hanging off the cliff, what is it you refuse to allow yourself to see? When trying to assist someone else, you want to *gently* help the troubled person see the situation in a new way. By this, we do not mean criticize or point out their faults. This will not help. Instead, use questions or personal observations to kindly draw attention to the area being overlooked. Please realize that these "hidden" options may seem perfectly obvious to you. Nudges almost always work significantly better than pushing hard. Questions are often very effective. If handled well, the troubled person seems to "discover" the best option independently. When they succeed in making the internal shift of energy, a huge boost in self-esteem and personal power often occurs. Notice that what is hidden from the negative person's view is usually where all the "juicy" lessons and issues can be found.

3. *Take it slow.* Don't let impending crisis trigger feelings of panic and anxiety. A slow, careful pace is the most secure way to climb to safety. When helping a troubled person, maintain a calm and gentle tone of voice, no matter the tone of the negative person. Consciously and deliberately slow the pace of the conversation. This will reduce any tension in the situation. Begin with small action plans: small goals with quick, successful outcomes. It's important that these are *team plans,* too. You might say, for example, "Let's sit down and talk about this over a cup of tea" or "Let's write down the important points you're making. It may help you see a potential solution."

4. *Make a deliberate choice about what to mirror.* If you are feeling negative, you can deliberately choose to mirror the energy of someone who is neutral or positive. If you're trying to help someone else, deliberately choose *not* to mirror the negative energy. Mirroring is a doorway to intimacy, useful when two people want to get closer. In a negative situation, however, mirroring makes things worse, so you must take deliberate action to break the habit of *always* mirroring someone close to you. Learn to use conscious mirroring. Experiment with this by doing some intentional mirroring or counter-mirroring (which means to reflect energy that is opposite what you receive). Situations to practice are easy to find: a grumpy salesclerk, an impatient shopper, or an angry child. In each case, the easiest reaction is to return the negative energy. "Fight fire with fire," as they say. We suggest that you deliberately practice using water on the fire instead. Try to figure out what the opposite energy is, and intentionally use counter-mirroring in an attempt to diffuse the negative energy into neutral. In some circumstances you may try deliberately using neutral responses to negative. This tends to maintain the initial level—not increasing the negative, but usually not increasing the positive either. To truly neutralize a negative situation, you must use the opposite energy—yin against yang.

5. *Detach yourself from the outcome.* As long as you hold a strong negative energy charge on a particular outcome, you keep it high on the list of probabilities. The least probable outcome has the strongest neutral energy on it, strangely enough. Often, the strong energy *against* something is more intense than any strong energy *for* something. Both work as magnets drawing those outcomes to you. If you are the one feeling negative, detaching is often very difficult, for these are your own issues—things that are important to you. Detaching tends to be much easier when helping another person. With close companions or relatives, you may be

surprised at how much attachment you have to a particular outcome. It is very helpful to the troubled person if you can give complete permission for any outcome. You may ask, "How can I detach from an outcome I don't want?" Try to uncover the core fear that triggers your strong reaction. That fear is where this attachment is hooked to your energy system. The core fear often seems to be unrelated to the current issue. You bypass layers of superficial issues by going straight to the core fear. This fear is usually tied to abandonment and self-esteem issues, which relate to your human search for unconditional love from others and from yourself. Release a core fear and many attachments fall away automatically. Observing your attachments helps you to locate your core fears. Also, remember that neutral is the opposite of desire for something; a strong negative feeling of *not* wanting a particular outcome operates on an energy level as another form of desire.

When you are the one hanging from the cliff:
   * Seek out someone who is solidly positive.
   * Don't get stuck in relating every little negative detail.
   * Focus on a solution, not just the problem.
   * In positive times, establish partnerships for mutual support.
   * Do your best alone before turning to another.
   * Don't just talk; listen carefully to the other person's responses.
   * If you can, take a walk alone right after sharing.
   * Feel free to gently reject suggestions, but keep an open mind.

When you are trying to help someone else:
   * Make sure you are not feeling negative, too.
   * Ask questions that lead to deeper issues.
   * Use neutral or positive language only.

* Don't reinforce complaints.

* Don't criticize or lecture.

* Try to look beyond the surface of the details.

* Use a broad perspective; share what you see.

* Look for honest positives to reinforce and strengthen.

* Don't feel responsible to fix things for them.

* Try to help them see things from a different angle.

* Speak calmly, gently, and slowly.

* Take the lead in setting the tone of the interaction.

* Speak from your heart.

* Breathe slowly and deeply. (They'll follow your lead.)

Part C – Manifesting

Manifesting is one of the most practical and useful applications for energy work. Following are several ways to add energy and speed to your desires. As you may realize, energy work is the underlying source for the power of prayer. Thoughts become reality. Focused thought manifests your desires out there in the future; you must move through time and space to reach them. Hopefully, you control your thoughts well enough that you do not manifest the state of "not having." If you focus your thoughts on what you lack, *more* of that lack is what you end up with! Your desires are manifested more solidly out there in the future when you layer the creative energy in multiple applications.

Your desires reach you more quickly when fueled by strong emotion. If you think of something you *do* want with strong emotion, you get more of it faster. However, if you think about something you *do not* want with strong emotion (like fear), you also get more of it faster! When your planet was still operating at 10 mph, the time lag was so long, it was more difficult to connect thoughts with consequences. At the current speed, your thoughts may bring almost instantaneous results. Uncontrolled thought causes difficulty for you in two ways: manifestation of negative creations and erasure of positive creations. From our perspective, we see a creation moving toward you through time and space. Suddenly, POUF! Your creation disappears as soon as you think about how impossible it is. When this happens, you disbelieve that you can manifest from thoughts because sometimes you can't see the results. When you leave your house for work, you don't disbelieve that your office will be there just because you cannot see it from your house! Indeed, your office will not be there, however, if you take a wrong turn along the way. With manifesting, you must stay on the road, moving through time and space, in order to reach your creations. Over time, you may notice a "click" when your creation is so solidly in place that it would be very difficult to erase it. This signifies increasing ability at manifesting.

Each day, you constantly manifest with your thoughts. We suggest that you work at eliminating negative thoughts altogether, even if that means you think about neutral things most of the time. Then, from time to time, focus your thinking on your goals and desires in order to consciously and deliberately manifest what you want. This is particularly powerful if it is not "erased" for several hours, so it is helpful to send out your thought-desires with a lot of positive emotion right before you sleep at night. (Rather like saying your prayers!) As the hours pass while you sleep, you will not think negatively.

Energy Circles

If you want to add tremendous energy to your desires, you can use Energy Circles. This is a group technique, for a gathering of three to eight people. It is most effective with five or seven persons in the group, but it works fine with a few less or a few more. With more than eight people, the energy gets rather large and hard to handle. It's also more difficult for a large group to maintain a tight focus, which is very important.

The energy output of the group is *multiplied* rather than simply cumulated, meaning a linked group of five people increases to the energy equivalent of 25 individual people! For this reason, it is *critical* that the group have an overwhelmingly positive energy overall! You can offset negative energy from one person (someone who may be sick or out of work, for instance), but the majority of the group needs to be in a state of "want" rather than "need." Desperate people focus on what they lack, and an entire group of people like this will strongly energize more of the scarcity! Allow the universe to help you form the group. If someone forgets to come or can't make it that night, perhaps it is to help balance the energy of the group as a whole. Select a leader for the evening, or take turns serving as leader. Once your Energy Circle is gathered, there are three components to the technique:

1. One person explains his/her desire or intention to the others. Group members create their own clear, focused mental images of the intention to energize. Different images are okay, as group members create images meaningful to themselves. The *vital* ingredient to this component is to clearly communicate the desire to everyone. This step may take only a minute or two; however, questions and qualifications are encouraged.

2. Seated in a circle, the group joins hands. It does not matter if you sit on the floor or on chairs. The leader directs the group to close their eyes and focus on the intention just discussed. After a couple of deep breaths, the group leader says "Begin." Energy moves around the circle in a clock-wise manner, getting stronger and stronger before peaking and then decreasing in intensity. The group leader breaks the linking of hands and says, "OK." This part does not take a lot of time—fifteen to thirty seconds in all.

3. Each person in the group shares any changes in their visual image during the energizing. Many people have definite "visions" occur during the intense energy movement. These can be very literal, but often the images come in metaphors, like dreams. You need a good understanding of dream metaphors to decipher some of them. People may see differing images that make more sense when everyone has shared his/her own experience. It's fine to jump around the circle in a random order to share these. Don't be surprised if several people see similar things. This important part of the process may trigger more excitement than the actual energizing! When listening to all the images, the person with the energized intention may experience a sense of intense pleasure. Listening to all the visualizations, the desire seems more real by the moment! This helps that person to "allow" the desire to come into their life. This step takes five to ten minutes or longer.

Repeat these three steps for each person's intention. For a group of five to seven people, the whole process generally takes a couple of hours. You're likely to find a great deal of humor naturally interwoven in the process. A magic of sorts comes from the fun and laughter. From our perspective, it "opens" everyone and allows more energy to flow. When you are having fun, you are energizing at a high level. You will feel energetic and "up" at the end of the Energy Circle. Rather than form a permanent group, we recommend that you keep this an open process with different people at different times. Also, let your intuition guide you on frequency. This is so powerful, you may consider doing it monthly rather than weekly. Allow the group energy to "hold" on one particular batch of desires for a little while. An Energy Circle is a powerful technique that uses growth with joy. When you try it, don't forget the laughter!

Truly Positive Statements

Feel free to be creative about energizing your goals, using any method or combination of methods that pleases you. In fact, this is a particularly powerful time to strengthen your focus on your wishes and desires since the additional energy brings them to you more quickly and with more intensity. However, it is crucial to be in a completely *positive* focus, or you will be getting what you *don't* want equally as quickly and with more intensity! Be alert to deceptively negative thoughts and affirmations that actually focus your mind on the opposite of what you truly want. Be quite conscious of this until you have developed enough skill to recognize it when you come across one, in yourself and others. Some illustrations of such deceptive statements follow, with a truly positive form of the same statement:

> *Deceptively negative:* "I want out of my stinking job." (This will get you *more* of that hated job.)
>
> *Truly positive:* "I want a harmonic shift into a new job, where I'm well-paid to do something I love so much I would do it for free!"
>
> *Deceptively negative:* "I want to quit feeling so physically bad."
>
> *Truly positive:* "I want to feel glowing good health. I enjoy being in physical form; my body gives me pleasure."

Notice that the truly positive statements have no indication of a problem to be eliminated. At the outset, it is often difficult to *think* in a truly positive manner when you're *feeling* bad or negative. Remember that neutral is your goal at that time. "I want to feel neutral," becomes your intention when in negative. Once that is achieved, the truly positive goal becomes clearer and more attainable. It is often helpful to use the word "harmony" in your goal statements. When things come to you "in a harmonic way," there is a gentle transition. Harmony works to smooth bumps in the road between you and your goal. Harmony brings things to you in pleasant ways. For instance, you may want to intend money come to you "from any harmonic source," or else you may get lots of money, but from a traumatic car accident that pays a big settlement!

Part D – Channeling

The Basics

In order to move smoothly through upcoming years, each of you need to develop a strong connection to your Higher Self and your other guides. One aspect of energy work is learning how to open yourself to these higher energies. Over time, as you gain information and experience, you will find yourself channeling whatever information you need to move through a lesson or situation. Each person reading this book has guides waiting, available to assist you whenever you open to their energy. These guides will not push their way into your consciousness; you must willingly invite the energy, so there is nothing to fear about this process. Our purpose is to provide enough knowledge of the techniques and the sensations of the process to allow you to "plug in" easily and smoothly.

Higher guidance is your goal, and high guides have a particular feeling or way of doing things that is easily recognized. Much like sex education teachers on your planet, we guides must use great care to provide appropriate information at the best time, without ruining things by giving you too much, too soon. Our primary guideline is to offer helpful information without overly-influencing your choices and decisions. High guides are not interested in controlling your actions or judging your behavior. High guides will not tell you what you "should" do, except in the context of "If you want this outcome, this choice will tend to move you in that direction." If you ever accidently get connected to a lower energy, you can easily recognize the difference. Any energy who seeks to scare you by making wild, frightening predictions is not the higher guidance you seek. We are not speaking of "evil entities"—just energies operating from fear. Don't even bother to tell this kind to "go away," as that is attention which continues to feed it energy and keeps it around longer. Without acknowledging the lower energy anymore, simply intend to connect with the highest guidance possible. There is nothing you need to learn right now from these fearful beings.

There is a simple technical reason for interference of this sort: between you and your high guides is a layer of choppy, erratic energy on the Astral Plane. This is where souls go between incarnations, regardless of how evolved they are. For this reason, the "garbage" information that new channels tend to get, comes from the messy energy on the Astral Plane. This erratic energy, coming from very young souls with only a few lifetimes of experience, works like static interference on the radio. It hinders clear reception of the energy from higher sources. In order to get a strong connection to your guides, you must learn to take your personal energy higher, stretching beyond the static of the Astral Plane. Channeling is really like being an extension cord, bringing the energy from the wall to the lamp where it's needed. The difficulty for your guides is this: How do they teach you to reach them until you've already figured out how to reach them? Their solution has often been to use a trusted older soul who is currently on the Astral Plane as a middle-man, who then transmits the information from a lower position that can more easily reach you. Of course, there is more static interference in this situation, until you learn how to modulate your energy into a pattern that plugs into the high guides directly.

During the initial phase of the connecting process, the information itself may be questionable at times due to the static affecting the quality of the reception. Don't worry if you some-times get garbled or overly-simplistic answers. At this point, your goal is to get whatever answers you can with whatever technique seems to work best. The process and system is being "installed," and you are not yet operating at full capacity. Expect a period of a few weeks to a few months to complete this phase. Your guides will move you along at the fastest pace possible, without jolting you with anything that will frighten you. A playful attitude is best. Lower energies are drawn to fear and pain much more than joy and playfulness. Having fun is your best defense against "junk" energies.

There are a variety of channeling methods and techniques. Some will immediately be more magnetic to you, but feel free to try each type as an experiment. Most channels find that certain meth-ods give certain types of information more clearly. Among the various ways to channel that we present, you will likely find more than one that is easy for you. Most musicians find that proficiency on one instrument leads to easily-developed skillfulness on other instruments. If you have several channeling techniques to choose from, you can use whichever type best suits the situation or the question. For many of you, there is a need for a *very* well-devel-oped intuitive ability. Some of you will even be teaching this type of information to others, so you need a well-rounded understand-ing of all areas and methods.

Now for some technical information about channeling: You need energy flowing smoothly into certain parts of your body to receive the energy and transform it into some form of answer. Be-cause the information travels on your own internal energy system, you must have strong energy flow to certain areas of your system to use certain forms of channeling. For instance, pendulums and dowsing rods require only minimal energy moving to the hands from the fourth chakra. Some channeling methods require that the energy move in a pattern, operating in two areas in an alternat-ing fashion. (e.g. Automatic writing requires energy in the hand (fourth chakra) and in the brain (seventh chakra). If you have difficulty with a method, observe your energy system and be sure you have clear pipelines to the required areas.

Your high guides are seeking to use minimal amounts of energy in their work with you. Many new channels marvel at the delicacy of the energy. In fact, most of you have actually been channeling for many years. You just never recognized that the soft little feeling, image or voice was not your own. As you quiet your own noisy thought processes, you begin to sense the different feeling of your guides' energy. Knowing how to meditate is not a requirement in order to channel, however the ability to quiet your mind can speed the connecting phase. *Tip:* If you already meditate, don't go all the way into a deep meditation. Your goal is to reach silence, rather than nothingness. You need to stay aware enough to receive the answers or information.

✧ *Pendulum/Dowsing:* The two most basic forms of channeling are pendulums and dowsing rods. These can even be used by people who have significant energy blockages, especially in the fifth chakra and above. You need only a tiny bit of energy moving through the fourth chakra, into the arms and then the hands. If you have strong personal energy flow, you might have a little trouble with these until you reduce the flow to the hands. (Imagine volume knobs on the wrists and turn them down to the level that works best.) These methods work best when you seek a yes or no answer. There are strong limitations to these methods when you need complex answers. The questions must be asked with precision or you will misinterpret the answers. For this reason, we are not going to spend much time on these methods. However, there are some isolated times that a pendulum or dowsing rods may be most useful; feel free to play with them if you like. They can be lots of fun! For instance, dowsing rods can help you pinpoint energy "hot spots" in your home. Most rooms have at least one of these columns of particularly strong energy. You may finally understand why the dog always sleeps in that certain place.

✧ *Guided Imagery:* This technique is an extension of the visual images you have been using to modulate your energy. You need energy moving into the seventh chakra, but only a small quantity. This method uses very little energy because there is no physical plane manipulation needed. Everything is happening outside physical reality. Also, this technique uses the most basic "language" of the Universe: the metaphor. Images carry many more layers of messages than words. However, you must understand the meaning of the metaphors for this method to work for you. Many other types of channeling involve the interpretation of metaphors—astrology, tarot cards, numerology, and more. If you do not already understand the metaphors in dreams or poetry, you will need a little study to use this method. A good source book is *The Dream Book* by Betty Bethards; it is an extensive, channeled list of metaphors and their meanings.

The Temple

Try this extended visualization. Travel up in the mountains, higher and higher, through beautiful woods and past cool, clear water courses. Focus all your physical senses into the image in order to shift your consciousness completely; touch the trees, smell the flowers, listen to the birds. When you reach a large structure called "The Temple," knock on the door and one of your guides will answer. This person may be male or female, old or young, a beautiful goddess or a hunched librarian. If you have trouble, just "create" the needed person or thing with your mind. At some point, these visualizations tend to take on a life of their own. You can move from room to room in the Temple—into the library, the chapel, or the art museum. It has many rooms to explore. Ask your guide to explain anything you see. You can ask about past lives; there's even a movie theater there where you can see movies of previous incarnations! Don't forget to look at your lifeplan, the blueprint for this lifetime.

Depending on the individual, a guide may "show" the information; for others, the guide may be more verbal. In either case, you can ask questions about anything. Sometimes you may have specific questions, and other times you may want to roam around and see what you can find that's interesting. Either way, your guides will pull you to whatever will be most helpful. Play with this technique and you may be surprised at the easy, quick results you get.

✧ *Automatic Writing:* This is a very good option for almost all of you. It is an extremely energy-efficient technique. It is also very private and easy to access even in a public place (like on an airplane or at your desk at work). Sometimes you need to "talk to someone" right then, and a pendulum or a deck of Tarot cards might not be appropriate! In this category, we group together two types of automatic writing, both handwritten and typewritten channeling. Start with the typing first, but only if your typing skills are natural and flowing. If you must "think" about the typing, it will get in the way of your channeling.

When you use automatic writing, some energy must flow through the entire chakra system. A small thread of energy into the brain and seventh chakra is necessary, as this is what creates efficiency in this method. Another small thread of energy flows to your hand (for writing) or both hands (for typing). Large quantities of energy would be required to manipulate your entire hand, but little energy is needed when your "auto-pilot" for writing is activated. Notice that when you write (or type) quickly, your thoughts are on the content rather than the physical act itself. While automatic writing, your hand or fingers are activated only to help you "find" the rest of the message which is "popped" into your brain by the energy flowing there. The technical term for what happens in your head is "brain impingement," and it feels like a thought bubble has been put into your brain. When it "pops," you experience a complete knowingness of a word, an entire phrase, an image, sometimes a complete conceptual focus that can be quite complicated. It feels similar to when you suddenly remember something you've been trying to pull out of the cobwebs of your brain. One moment it's not there, the next moment it is. Carol reports to us that it is actually a very pleasant sensation, once you get used to letting it happen.

There are several processes that occur as you and your guides prepare to communicate through automatic writing. First, practice moving energy to the hands and the brain. If there are any major energy blockages, it's okay, you need only get a thread up to the seventh chakra. Energy has a distinctive feeling, perhaps a tingling or vibrating sensation. Your guides will send their messages in with additional high-grade energy they will layer onto your own energy flow. It is critical that you elevate your own energy to the highest level you can reach. Using visualization and/or music, practice going higher and higher, for that is how you get past the clutter of the Astral Plane. Don't worry yet about writing; just play with the sensation and get comfortable with the feeling of the energy.

In the next stage of interaction, most people have a period of time where their guides do most of the work! There is a "brain-mapping" process, where your guides poke around to see how you set up your mental filing systems. They study your personal vocabulary and the nuances of meaning around each word that you use. They map the neural connectors in your brain, to create efficient and meaningful communications with you. This stage occurs only with your permission and encouragement. At times, it may happen with the approval of your Higher Self only, but most guides wait until you are fully aware and invite them in. You feel no discomfort, just a sensation of energy flowing into your brain. There is a tingling sensation in the head, sometimes like someone is "tinkering" around up there. Even as this period continues, you can easily initiate the third phase, where you start to get information and answers from your guides.

People often begin writing with simple, repetitive movements, particularly spirals and figure-8 shapes. These serve to build up the energy flow to the hand. At the typewriter or computer, this may occur as rhythmic typing of the same letters over and over—like FJFJFJFJ. This is just warm-up, like a jogger does on a cold morning. At first, you may find the information is quite general, sometimes flowery and not as specific as you might desire. Be patient, because your guides are probably working on the process more than the content at this early stage. Write whatever pops into your head. Your hand may start writing the first letter just before your head knows what the word is.

If you have specific questions, we suggest that you write them all down at one time. Then, sit down with that list and let the answers flow unbroken. Mental gymnastics are needed to shift back and forth from sending out the questions and receiving the answers. Later, this gets easier to do, but it is troublesome for beginners. Simply let the information flow out onto the page. Don't judge it while you write it; leave that for later. Activating the judgement sections of your brain during the transmission tends to block the flow. If you find yourself judging the value of some information, just tell yourself to look at it later. Particularly at first, we highly recommend that you go back and look over the material after a day or two (or longer). Until you are clearly comfortable with the process and the information you are getting, don't make any major life decisions based on your channeling. Your high guides always moderate what they give you, matching it to your level, so initial information is often purposely vague. This keeps you from giving the guides too much power over your decisions. You may also get some astral clutter mixed in with valuable information at this stage. Over time, you learn to discern the difference, and the quality of your channeling will escalate.

During this channeling process, you are in a light trance caused by the high-grade energy that flows from your guides. What you write seems obvious and even simplistic to you *as you write it*. However, when you read it later, back in your normal state of consciousness, you may react differently. It may seem newer and fresher to you. The information you get while using automatic writing will seem like "yours" as you do it; only later does it become apparent that there is great depth to the information. You may find it valuable to reread your channeled information several times, for high guides sometimes layer information in cunning ways, putting in things that you don't notice at first. Later, when you reach another level of understanding, you often find lots of new stuff in older writings.

Good channeling is very energy-efficient. Many new channels comment on how delicate and light the energy is. You may need to adjust your belief system on this subject in order to recognize energy that has been flowing through you for a long time. For most of you, higher guides are "knocking at your door" and have been for some time. This will be much easier than you thought. Just open the door and invite them in, and your guides will do most of the work. You will do best by having an attitude of playfulness toward this skill.

✧ *Other Channeling Methods:* Your guides can get information to you in many ways. Ouija board, tarot cards, trance-channeling, even crystal balls and candle-gazing have some ardent users who glean much insight from these tools. We choose not to spend time explaining all these methods because they are all much less efficient than the techniques already discussed in this section. If you like, feel free to experiment with any and all channeling methods. The new planetary energy makes it significantly easier to get in touch with your guides, no matter what tool you use.

Part E – Other Tidbits

We conclude this chapter with some odds and ends about energy in general, and how to regulate your personal energy flow. These bits and pieces of information vary in subject-matter and may lack some cohesiveness here, but each of you will likely find at least one that proves truly helpful.

✧ *Handling Stress:* With the intensified planetary energies, you probably find yourself under stress from time to time. You may also sense a great deal of stress in people around you—family, friends, even strangers like fellow shoppers and store clerks. First, you need to develop an internal signal that makes you aware of your personal stress level whenever it grows from a low level into a moderate level. *Do not* allow yourself to reach high stress levels; even a short burst of such intense energy will likely disrupt your personal energy flow for at least 24 hours, perhaps as long as a week! This is caused by the new stronger energy on your planet. Use good judgement as you observe your own stress levels, and take a little time out for a soothing cup of herbal tea or a protein snack. Even moderate levels of stress deplete your non-physical *and* physical energy, so pay attention to your energy system as a whole. As you sit quietly for 15-20 minutes with your tea and crumpets (or whatever), do a brief, one or two minute meditation. Even in a public place, you can find an object to focus on in your environment (a plant, a photograph in a magazine, an advertisement or sign), and use your deep breathing as you shut out all other thoughts for a minute or so. Then, finish by visualizing yourself feeling calm and happy at the end of your task at hand (work, shopping trip, cookie-baking session, whatever...). This is a helpful technique to use when you're standing in a *long* line. Just be sure to get back to current reality by the time the clerk waits on you! You will be amazed at how much better you feel at the end of the day. Intensify your little "mini-meditations" for any high stress period like the holidays or a busy time of year at work. It's a good habit to develop. Use it as needed.

✧ *Dream Messages:* Currently, each of you complete tremendous amounts of work at night while you're sleeping! You leave your body in order to travel around and work with others as you make adjustments and coordinate lifeplans. If you want to track the work, simply pay more attention to your dreams. Please be patient with yourself if you sometimes need a bit more sleep than usual (whether at night or occasional naps). There is a lot to be done in the space of only a few short years, which is a tight schedule from a cosmic point of view. As we mentioned earlier, you need to understand the *language* of dreams in order to get the messages from the dreams. Do some research into dream metaphors through books or other sources. Although you have your own unique message system to decode, it almost certainly uses the basic metaphors common to your entire species.

✧ *Energy "Spiking":* This is a new term, referring to a phenomenon that is beginning to happen with more frequency now that the planetary energy is so strong and fast. When your energy "spikes," you experience a sudden burst of strong energy that lasts for a short time. It may sustain for just seconds or minutes, but for a few people it can last several hours. An average length of time is twenty to thirty minutes. The sensation is strong but pleasant if your chakras are open; you may feel warm, even a sort of "hot flash," but it is never disruptive or frightening once you understand what is happening. However, if you have a blockage or a closed-off section within your system, you may feel some discomfort in the area that's blocked. Use whatever method works best for you personally, eliminating the excess energy from *below* the blockage point. (Usually, this will be a draining process through the lower part of your body; second or third chakras, especially.) Even after the energy spike itself has ended, you may still need to rinse out excess energy that's stuck at the blockage point. Walking, sexual activity, or a warm bath are options to consider. (Of course, you want to make sure timing is appropriate for any of these methods!) The cause for an energy spike is within the planetary energy flow, which is not flowing at a regular pace yet. The energy flow into the planet ebbs at times, but it is not very noticeable; when a gushing surge of energy hits your system, *that* you cannot miss!

✦ *Regular Energy "Workouts":* Most of you are familiar with the favorable results that come from regular exercise—aerobics, jogging, walking, etc. Regular energy "workouts" can have the same kind of positive results. The closest physical comparison is weight-lifting, which builds strength and muscle from continued small incremental increases over a moderate amount of time. Energy workouts enlarge your energy flow and your aura size, particularly when you follow a regulated schedule. The frequency and length of your energy workout is just as individual as a weight-lifter's workout. You must use your own intuition to find what feels best to you. When you hit the most harmonic workout pattern, you'll definitely feel energized and intensely alive! Too few or too many workouts in a short period of time can leave you either tired or wired, tossed about on the waves of planetary energy that are crashing on your head these days. In fact, you may experience both of these in sequence, feeling very hyper or tense followed by an energy crash into exhaustion or mild depression. The point of the energy workout is to fully energize your system, opening all the valves (chakras) as widely as possible under your own focused attention. Exact methodology is not the point here; you may use any technique that pleases you, adjusting the method from one workout to the next. Try to establish a routine time and place for some kind of energy workout that fully charges your energy batteries. If you want your energy system to look like Arnold Schwarzenegger's body, you must approach your workouts with a great deal of structure and planning (with regular frequency). Like exercising your body, if you simply want to maintain a healthy energy system, you won't need to "workout" as much as a professional body builder needs to do. As always, the choice is yours.

✧ *What's Knocking at Your Door?* In a humorous contradiction to the *routine* we just suggested, we now advise that you work to loosen up some of the more routine areas of your life. Habits and routines can sometimes be blockages to allowing new things into your daily activities. New "stuff" might include new people, new interests, or even new work—and all these new things are probably connected to your lifeplan! When a rigid lifestyle closes the door on the face of important lifeplan work, you will get loud knocking on that door! Now is an excellent time to look around your life, checking to see if you are ignoring something that is trying to get in. The simplest way to let these new things flow into your life is to maintain a deliberate awareness of your actions, allowing your Higher Self to signal you if some change in the regular routine is helpful at a particular point. When you move through your day in a sort of "waking sleep," following your normal routine, you may be missing some signals and losing efficiency in your plans. Simply ask yourself this question during your day: "Am I doing this (. . . wearing this, eating this, saying this . . .) because it's habit, or is it truly what I want most right now? Investigate your other choices, and how they compare to the choice you're making. What do you want? In this way, you never feel forced into any changes . . . you simply activate a change in habit at the earliest opportunity, through conscious awareness and deliberate action.

✧ *Love or Fear?* During each day, you make thousands and thousands of individual decisions and choices. *Every single choice can be used to increase love in your life.* Of course, you may use your choices to increase the fear in your life as well. At times, it can be difficult to figure out which is which! Ultimately, this continuous flow of choices is why you are here. Certainly, you often have big decisions that can cause huge consequences in your life, but those are dwarfed by the sheer numbers of small choices made day in and day out. Most of you work very hard on those few big decisions, and hardly think about the exorbitant number of small ones each day. Reverse that energy! Spend more time focusing on the little things, and you will find that the large choices work themselves out quite nicely. Develop good "choosing habits" —by this we mean to train yourself to recognize love . . . and then always choose it! Like most skills, repetition and practice are needed for you to feel completely confident in your choosing abilities. Start now. Choose love over fear at this moment . . . and in every other moment for the rest of your life.

Chapter Fourteen

Universal Energy Laws

There are Universal Laws at work, based on the functions of energy. Here is a short summary of these laws, followed later in the chapter by an expanded explanation of each.

Law 1: The Law of Attraction
Energy of any form magnetically attracts similar energy. Intense emotion causes a more intense attraction in both speed and quantity.

Law 2: The Law of Polarity
Energy always contains a duality or polarity. This may be seen as positive/negative, male/female, good/bad, high quality/low quality. This creates an unending array of choices within choices as you select your preferred polarity at each crossroad.

Law 3: The Law of Neutrality
Perfectly matched polarities create a state of neutrality, providing a third choice outside the two polarities of any energy.

Law 4: The Law of Consequences
Within the physical plane, energy moves through time and space. Energy always touches other energies, creating reactions, and thus, consequences. (This applies to energy within the time/space continuum. Adjustments to the law are needed for outside the physical plane.)

Law 5: The Law of Intention
Intentional energy is condensed and magnified. Energy tends to move in all directions at once, but it can be focused and aimed with conscious intent. Intention influences energy going out, as well as the energy magnetically attracted back.

Law 6: The Law of Allowing
General energy moves into open pathways only, stopping or moving around blockages. Intentional energy can open a closed pathway, but only when allowed by a change in preference.

Law 7: The Law of Universality
All is available. All flows around you at every moment, but you experience only what you prefer. The Universe reflects you, and you reflect the Universe. All is.

As you can see, these laws are generalities which influence every part of existence. If you use specific methods and techniques, you can put the energies of the Universe to work for you to fulfill your desires. But first, you make fundamental choices as you select a *basic soul preference* that influences you for many lifetimes. This choice leads to *lifetime goals* for your current incarnation, and those goals lead to *daily choices*. There is a basic soul preference at work in the world today: growth with pain versus growth with joy. This is your first decision. *Please* clearly state your preference between the two; to yourself, to other people, to God, to the Universe, to All That Is.

Many of you are still wavering or shifting back and forth on this important choice. You continually change your decision from day to day, even minute to minute. Once you clearly focus on the pathway of growth with joy, you find a fundamental shift in your perspective on life. Your guides, your own Higher Self, your angels all turn their attention to seeking the joyful pathway. New sources of happiness come into your life—people, experiences, ideas, plans, events, etc. If you have any closed area in your energy system, some part of you that does not allow joyful energy in, you will discover where it is and how to open up that doorway. *Everything begins once you make this choice. What do you prefer?*

Universal Laws in Detail

Law 1: The Law of Attraction

Energy of any form magnetically attracts similar energy. Intense emotion causes a more intense attraction in both speed and quantity.

Most of you understand that what you think about is what you draw to yourself. Have you noticed how much faster this law is working these days? You may be unknowingly using the Law of Attraction to attract energy that is precisely what you do not want! To use this law most effectively, you need to understand the language of energy. Unlike your spoken and written languages on Earth, "Energy-speak" has only the noun attached to an energy magnet that draws in the matching energy. The only verb is "want." Your emotions fuel the magnetism, since strong feelings about something denotes a need to complete lessons in that area. The more you need to complete a particular lesson, the stronger your feelings will be about that subject (whether painful or joyful).

In "Energy-speak," any object, event, word, image, thought or feeling is representative of a certain energy, but it contains the *entire* energy of that item, the complete polarity. (More about this in Law 2.) Every energy has a duality, often called positive or negative. The Universe does not send you only half the energy. You get the entire package, and then *you* must select the aspect which you prefer from those two polarities. In this way, the Universe senses the energy itself rather than any extra message you attach. The Universe simply hears your preference for X over Y or Z, receiving only the energy of your thought. Like a mirror, energies that match what you send out will come reflecting back to you, growing in magnitude on the return trip. Remember, Universal Energy has no preference because all energies flow within it at all times. Here are some examples to illustrate:

"Don't send me X" . . . becomes . . . *"I want X."*

"I'm afraid of Y" . . . becomes . . . *"I want Y" (with a side order of more fear!)*

"I want a little bit of Z, but not too much" . . . becomes . . . *"I want Z."*

At all times, energy of every type flows around you. By thinking about "Z," you select a "Z" magnet that attracts "Z" energy. You control what you get by choosing your magnet, for everything is available at all times. Each individual thought is a small magnet. Repeated thoughts bring in matching energies that enlarge and compile over time into a larger, more powerful magnet. Thought patterns like this can be very strong because of the number of repetitions, even if strong emotion is not involved. Any strong emotion immediately intensifies the power of your magnet, however. Even a small magnet from a single thought can become very strong with passionate emotion to escalate its magnetic pull. How do you manage your magnets for maximum, positive, joyful energy? It can be difficult to maintain positive, joyful thoughts at all times, so here are some tips.

1. *Notice your thoughts.* If asked, your Higher Self will notify you whenever you pick up a magnet that is incongruent with your intention for growth with joy. This is commonly a physical message, usually a knot in your stomach. (However, a secret code of any sort can be used as a signal between you and your Higher Self.) The hardest part of deliberate joy is *noticing* the unwanted "energy magnets" amidst all the thousands of intentions used each day.

2. *Replace unwanted thoughts with wanted ones.* Once you detect an unwanted thought magnetizing unwanted energy, simply ask yourself "What *do* I want regarding this topic?" This replaces the last request with a new request to the

Universe. Change your order, so to speak. If you're unsure what you want, simply intend clarity on the issue. Ask for more information about your choices, until you have enough input to know what you want.

3. *Learn how to recognize what you ask for.* Clarity is very important. Much of what you receive is murky and jumbled, because much of what you send out is that way. When you think in a confused, cluttered manner, you invite more confusion and clutter in your life. If you need clear and orderly thinking, intend clarity. Write out some of your intentions in order to evaluate their clarity. Simplification is always helpful.

Law 2: The Law of Polarity

Energy always contains a duality or polarity. This may be seen as positive/negative, male/female, good/bad, high quality/low quality. This creates an unending array of choices within choices as you select your preferred polarity at each crossroad.

Look around you and study the polarity of the physical plane. This is the basis for all preference, for if there were no differences between things, you could never choose! From a cosmic view, there is no better or worse—just choices. (Remember, the only value judgement in the Universe is energy efficiency. The "best" choice is that which uses the least amount of energy to achieve the goal.)

Some choices are like selecting a flavor of ice cream. Which is better, chocolate or vanilla? The answer depends on who is doing the choosing. Keep this in mind as you observe the choices of others. You can easily make judgements about other people's choices without having full knowledge of the situation. In many cases, they are simply choosing a growth pathway that is different from your own. Keep in mind that growth with pain is still a choice for growth.

Polarity creates pathways, similar to neural networks. "Energy-speak" has no isolated negatives or positives. Every choice is a complete energy package, containing full polarity. At this point, every energy you magnetize holds both joyful and painful aspects. *Any choice* can lead to joy or pain, depending on your next choice. *Every situation* contains the seeds for success or failure, depending on how you handle the next preference. In this zone, you are never completely lost and you are never completely safe.

Your soul maneuvers through a sea of choices over many hundreds of lifetimes. Without a *basic soul preference* by which to navigate, you would move about this ocean of choices in a random manner. With a strong fundamental intention for joyful growth, it becomes easier and easier to choose the most joyful polarity out of each energy that comes to you. Your pathway constantly forks in two directions, because of the polarities.

Your *basic soul preference* has been *growth* for thousands upon thousands of years. Because of the current energy shift on Earth, you have reached another crossroad—another choice. Until now, the choice between growth with pain or growth with joy was available, but not required. Today's intensified energy makes this a *necessary* choice. In fact, this is a planetary choice, determined by the sum of individual decisions. After many, many pro-joy choices, you ultimately enter a delightful energy zone where your decisions are no longer between pain or joy. From this place, you choose between *less* joy and *more* joy! Only after choosing less joy many, many times, would you reenter the pain/joy polarity.

You have another navigation tool available to you, useful over mid-length distances, when you become aware of your *lifetime goal* which is the end result of your lifeplan efforts. You already have an exciting goal for this lifetime. In fact, you spent tremendous amounts of energy working out complex plans and intricate agreements with other souls. These plans provide a strong magnetic pull for your entire group, keeping each of you on target as you move along together like a flotilla of ships. If you are not yet aware of your lifetime goal, let your higher guidance provide you with more information about it. Somewhere deep inside, you have a full and complete knowingness of the plan. Conscious awareness of your lifetime goal leads to conscious focus of your energy. This intensifies the energies you send out and magnetize back to yourself.

Whenever you have these larger navigation tools in place, you find *daily choices* becoming easier to make. At times, illogical twists and turns in your short-term pathway will occur. Allow yourself to move from crossroad to crossroad, knowing that a few mistaken turns will be easy to correct. Your overall direction will be clarified over time. The primary advantage of polarity is the steady movement it provides as you move from choice to choice, exercising your ability to prefer. This perpetual movement never leaves you entirely immobilized, for you can always make a new choice, change your preference, or try a different polarity on for size. Don't fight the flow of choices, because every "mistake" is just a pathway to another chance to choose.

Law 3: The Law of Neutrality

Perfectly matched polarities create a state of neutrality, providing a third choice outside the two polarities of any energy.

Some of you have an innate understanding of this law; others of you may draw a complete blank where this concept is concerned. Certain souls develop a preference for polarity only, ignoring neutrality. Some souls enjoy exploring neutral energy. There is no right or wrong here, as everyone eventually chooses to practice and learn about all Universal Laws. The order of your lessons comes from your own choosing. You cannot do it "wrong." These are some questions you may ask yourself as you attempt to gauge how much work you've already done in this area:

* Can you "step outside" physical or emotional pain?

* Is deep meditation fairly easy for you to achieve?

* Have you ever had an intentional out-of-body experience?

* Do you find it fairly easy to put aside judgmental thoughts?

* Have you ever deliberately made yourself invisible in an energy sense? (For example, as a student who did not know the answer, could you "hide" well enough that the teacher did not call on you?)

Each of these questions suggests a different aspect of *Neutral Energy*. Like all other forms of energy, neutral can be used well or poorly. First comes basic knowledge about neutral as an energy form, but later you need discernment to select when to use neutral and how long to maintain it. If you feel buffeted about by the experiences of your life, you may not be using neutral energy to soften some of the bumps in your road. Neutral operates like the shock absorbers on your car, cushioning the roughness of some sections of roadway. However, the main reason to understand neutral energy is because your neutral shock absorbers also help you go faster down the road! Right now, that is the most important benefit of using neutral energy. You need not spend so much time watching for rough spots in the road—you can concentrate on being on the right road, thinking about your destination ahead!

Neutral energy is used whenever you give equal preference to both sides of a polarity that faces you as a choice. It is not refusal to choose, nor is it allowing others to choose for you. Those are both very different in feeling and results. Neutral energy chooses both polarities equally, creating an energy loop that cancels itself out. Please note that most neutral energy loops maintain themselves only until your consciousness moves into a clear preference for one of the polarities. Neutral allows you to choose what you *do* want, instead of choosing the opposite of what you do not want. Neutral helps you go toward something joyful, instead of just away from something painful. Neutral is the fastest way to eliminate fear or pain. Not joyful itself, neutral is the doorway *to* joy.

Neutral energy is needed whenever you get confused, angry, fearful, sad, frustrated or tense. Sometimes your choices are influenced by self-limiting beliefs and negative thought patterns (thinking habits). These may lead to choices not aligned with your overall lifeplan. If you have a knot in your stomach, your Higher Self is using your emotions to let you know that your current thoughts are not in harmony with your lifetime goals. You have made a choice or choices which have moved your focus into growth with pain, instead of growth with joy. Neutral is the quickest and easiest way to shift your consciousness back in the direction of joy. After a little while in neutral, getting back to growth with joy is much simpler.

Neutral energy improves your perspective on life. You do not feel wonderful, but you do not feel bad either. You just *are*. Neutral is best used in short bursts; you may not want to spend years floating in neutral. Of course, some souls do just that. We are speaking here specifically to *you*, the White House group, who desire to attain higher levels of joyful energy than ever before at this level of the physical plane. Neutral energy helps you to keep advancing in your spiritual growth, using forward momentum that is unbroken by fear or pain energies.

Law 4: The Law of Consequences

Within the physical plane, energy moves through time and space. Energy always touches other energies, creating re-actions and thus consequences. (This applies to energy within the time/space continuum, and adjustments are needed when you step outside the physical plane.)

Sequence is part of your physical plane experience. If you do not connect your actions and outgoing energy with the results they engender, you will certainly have trouble with your life lessons. If you cannot figure out how you are creating your own problems, you will continue to experience the same issues time after time. Failure to connect a consequence to its source is why many people experience difficulty achieving joyful growth; this is also one rea-son that growth with pain has been effective for so long on your planet. Once you see the pattern and can predict outcomes, you race through many spiritual lessons. The intensification of planetary energy requires that you improve your understanding of this cosmic law. Before now, people on your planet have had a protective "buffer," or time lag, that lengthens the time from the original thought or action and its natural consequence. This gives you extra time to correct yourself, but it also makes it more difficult to connect the cause with the effect. The speeding up of Earth's core energy causes your consequences to come more quickly and with more intensity. You get *more* results *sooner*, even if you are unknowingly creating something that is painful. *Wake up* and start using your conscious will with awareness!

Your thoughts operate like nets thrown into the ocean. These "thought-nets" are permanently connected to you, their creator. Depending on the kind of net you throw out into the sea of universal energy, you capture a specific energy (health or illness, leadership or victimhood, pain or joy.) Your nets are always "harvested." It often seems like the contents are dumped right on your head at the moment you least expect it! You have had difficulty figuring out which "thought-net" caught which kind of "consequence-fish" because of the protective time lag. The reason for this time lag was to let you get used to things at a slower pace. If you jumped into instant consequences without being prepared by several hundred lifetimes of practice, you would think yourself dead many times over in only one day. (e.g. Some kind of near-miss auto accident, where you think "Wow, if I hadn't swerved, that big truck would have killed me!" Imagine yourself dead without a time lag—and you are!)

Of course, you still have a time lag today, but it is much shorter. We recommend greater care in your thought patterns, using your "gut reaction" to guide you as to whether you are in negative, positive or neutral. That knot in the pit of your stomach is a message from your Higher Self that you are sending out "thought-nets" for fish you don't want! Neutral helps you stop putting out any big nets for a little while. Certainly, conscious use of positive energy sends out big nets to quickly bring in the exact, perfect fish you desire.

Many times, you suddenly become aware that *something,* some kind of consequence, has been dumped on you, but you remain unaware of the source. Look beyond the current situation, further back in time, and seek out the point when the original thought-energy went out. Remember, before recent changes in planetary energy, this time frame may have been weeks or even years. For most of you, significant portions of your adult life are the consequences for decisions made between five and eighteen years of age. Sometimes this is obvious—like a 15-year old girl who has a baby. Sometimes it is not so obvious—like a 10-year old boy who never travels becoming an airline pilot, travelling constantly as an adult. Often what you *lack* as a child becomes what you unconsciously seek out in adulthood. The area of action/consequences is an important concept for children to learn as early as possible. Awareness is powerful at any age.

If you need work in this area, you may be feeling victimized by circumstances in your life. You tend to be constantly surprised by what happens to you, instead of being prepared in advance by intuitive and logical perceptions. There is no method better than experimentation to understand this law better. Consciously send out clear signals, then watch for the results. If you get something you don't understand, seek out the source. Some kind of lesson is usually attached. Remember, you can ask your guides for clarification. Throw out the "thought-net." What is the lesson in the situation? Your guides will send you "consequence-fish" of information and comprehension.

Ask for clarification if you *don't* get something you send out. You have a large supply of well-established thought patterns that have been habitual for a very long time. You may need to investigate these in order to clearly understand why you keep getting certain things in your life over and over. Start with a combination of "historical research" to find patterns, mixed with daily experimentation to practice sending out precise "thought-nets." Good fishing!

Law 5: The Law of Intention

Intentional energy is condensed and magnified. Energy tends to move in all directions at once, but it can be focused and aimed with conscious intent. Intention influences energy going out, as well as the energy magnetically attracted back.

Comprehension of this universal law is critical at this particular time. Operating in the dark, you may create a painful and unmanageable life for yourself. The energy shift causes all laws to become much more obvious, this one in particular. Look around and you'll easily see examples of this law at work in a negative way. Souls who feel completely victimized by the world around them can seldom understand how intention is at work in their lives. The strongest magnification of energy comes from strong emotion—positive or negative! Powerful fear of something is the most direct way to bring a large quantity of it quickly into your life.

When you focus your thoughts into the particular "shape" of some event (or object or situation), there is a tangible and measurable response from the Universe. Intention is a cookie-cutter, pulling a specific shape out of the undifferentiated cosmic energy that surrounds us all. Your intention is your personal cookie-cutter, so the shape it creates will arrive one day on the doorstep of your life. If the thought has strong intent, a nice firm push extracts a perfectly-shaped cookie in a single effort. (This is one reason Energy Circles can be very successful.) If the intent behind the thought is muddy with ambivalence, you may barely mark the cookie shape on top of the dough. Use repeated efforts with stronger intentions to extract your cookie, which may be somewhat misshapen if your cookie-cutter shape was a little different each time. In order to deliberately manifest joy into your life, you must have a good understanding of this law. To complete your plans for this lifetime, it takes more than simply *not* creating pain for yourself. Active use of intentional energy is the cornerstone of your journey to happiness. In order to efficiently use this law, you need to access your lifeplan, your goal, your dreams.

There is an untold amount of energy flowing through your physical form each day. Holding together a physical body is very energy-intensive! Energy flows in at the base of the system, and it flows out in all directions except when focused by your own intention. To us, you resemble water sprinklers as you send energy shooting out every which way! Then you wonder why everything around you is all wet! Occasionally, a clear strong intention sends a nice firm gush, right out the top of your head; this waters whatever particular "project-flower" you are trying to grow—and without causing people around you to need umbrellas! Deliberate intention allows you to become a more energy-efficient system.

Energy flows outward with aero-dynamic qualities. You may have experienced the sensation of having energy from another person pushing at you, perhaps probing to see how you react to something. Some people might hook in to your energy, sucking you dry. An emotionally-needy person commonly sends out energy lines in all directions, looking for some energy-rich source to plug into as a way to fill the low-energy levels of their own system. If you erect a barrier (a protective circle of white light around your body, for instance), you will feel buffeted by their pushing. You must expend energy to maintain the barrier too, so this is not very efficient. Another option is a conscious shaping of your own energy flow, sending a pointed thread of love-energy directly to the person's heart chakra. Just like the prow of a boat cutting through water, this sends the person's needy-energy hooks *around* your energy system. Your connection to this person can now be a loving one of your own creation, instead of a battleground, or an episode with an "energy vampire." Please realize that these are souls starving for energy or looking for combat. In either case, this technique makes you almost invisible to them. An added bonus is that their negative energy often becomes invisible to you.

The mindset of fighting off negatives increases the battles in your life. Never give energy and intention to what you do not want. Your goal is to see the possibility of positive at all times, in all things. We are not speaking of denial or a "Pollyanna" attitude, but a true realization of the lessons available. When you stop fighting with Life, it will stop fighting with you. When you shift your energy flow into a deliberate configuration of balance, you change *your own attitude* into a balanced form. What you experience is the manifestation of what your energy system is doing. Deliberate intent is the most powerful thing in the Universe.

Law 6: The Law of Allowing

General energy moves into open pathways only, stopping or moving around blockages. Intentional energy can open a closed pathway, but only when allowed by a change in preference.

This law speaks of the energy you allow to enter your system. You might be manifesting wonderful things for yourself, but are they sitting in your front yard because you will not open your front door to bring them into your house? You may need work in this area if you have worked hard at Law 5, but there is still nothing getting to you. If you currently have a high level of frustration, that is an important clue that non-allowance may be happening to you. Perhaps you feel as if you are sitting at a banquet, hungrily eyeing the aromatic food that lies just barely outside your reach. The more you work at manifesting, the more frustrated you become as more and more enticing food piles up on the banquet table . . . and you still cannot eat it. Very depressing, indeed!

Your energy system closes off "intake valves" whenever certain fears kick in. It may be a fear of change, a fear of loss, even a fear of doing harm to others. The act of opening this closed valve is not a tightening of the "soul-muscles" that *open*, for open is the natural state. Instead, it is a choice to feel safe and allow the normal open state to return. It is a choice to relax the "soul-muscles" that have contracted in fear. Think about the feeling when you will a muscle to relax. Notice how easily you forget to hold that relaxed state, but how simple it is to hold a slightly tensed state. This is the difficulty in allowing; you cannot actively think about *not* doing something without creating a message to yourself *to do* it. To allow, you must choose safety over danger. You choose love over fear. You choose joy over pain. If you change your preference, the feelings of safety, love and joy will open all blockages. Look closely at your intentions, observing anything that feels a little scary or strange to you. Remember that everything you desire can bring pain or joy to you. If blocked, your soul sees a big price tag attached that you are *not* willing to pay. Find out what negatives your perception has written on the price tag. Evaluate that particular item until you discover a new insight into it, or maybe you can figure out what you need to learn in order to feel safe with it. Sometimes the act of studying an item allows you to see that fear is unnecessary.

One more thing: you only feel the frustration of being blocked in this area if you are actively focusing your intentional energy. You never feel blocked from having something that you don't want. This may sound strange, but intense frustration at *not receiving* is a signal that you are sending out *powerful intentions!*

Law 7: The Law of Universality

All is available. All flows around you at every moment, but you experience only what you prefer. The Universe reflects you, and you reflect the Universe. All is.

An easy way to increase your ability to allow is to open yourself to Law 7. If you realize that everything you want is already there, you can release the need to struggle and overcome hardship. Why would it be necessary to pay a high price for something available in unlimited quantity? Abundance flows around you like a wide river with a perpetual source. The flow never stops; it will carry you along to wherever you wish without asking you to pay for a ticket. You must simply choose to enter the flow of the river by conscious intent. This is your choice, your preference. The only thing that shapes the Universe is your own perception of it.

Everything you observe around you is some aspect of yourself. Planetary conflicts and wars are all representative of internal battles within your own consciousness. Each brutal act of violence is a fearful, unloved part of yourself. Each act of kindness is part of you, too. Each earthquake is an outpouring of uncontrolled power, even rage, from within your own soul. Each heart-stopping spark of beauty in nature is also you. At your level of awareness, it can still be a difficult matter to understand the depth and breadth of your soul. It can also be hard to remember that you control it all by your choices. Can you choose to love it all? Can you choose light without needing darkness to find it? Can you let your soul's arms stretch wide enough to love all people, all creatures, all of nature? As you increase self-acceptance and self-love, your inner-directed love energy automatically brings more joy and light into the planet. In its most simple and elegant form, this is your lifeplan. Bringing light and love energies to the planet is what you came to do and why you are here. Whatever you can harmonize internally changes the externals on the planet. Look around at the world to study yourself.

Section Four

Onward and Upward

Chapter Fifteen

Current Influences

Astrological Influences

There are interesting and unique planetary influences occurring at this time. It is not our wish to provide a full course in astrology, but rather to focus on one occurrence–Saturn's return to Pisces on its normal thirty-year cycle. Saturn was in Pisces from April 1964 to March 1967. Some of you may recognize that time as the dawning of the "Peace Movement." It was a period filled with social transformation: flower children, mind-expansion through drugs or meditation, and the sexual revolution. Everyone who experienced the Pisces/Saturn energy of the '60's became attuned to this particular energy pattern. For many of you lightworkers, it influenced your basic belief patterns, shaping and preparing you for this particular time. Almost all of you experienced this energy in the 60's, even if it was in the womb.

On January 29, 1994, Saturn entered Pisces for the first time since the 1960's. Saturn represents your soul's chosen effort here on Earth, action taken within physical reality. It pulls forward hard work and challenge, especially in everyday actions and choices. Pisces represents the spiritual realm, with particular focus on your emotions. As the two energies blend, all persons on Earth feel a magnetism, an internal push into harmonic action that fulfills lifeplans. Saturn puts you to work, while Pisces keeps your heart and emotions involved. When these two energies intersect, you only feel comfortable with methods and behaviors that are harmonic and balanced for everyone involved, and yet there is also a cosmic compulsion to make progress. Balancing speedy progress and harmonic process is a juggling act for this energy combination.

Now, thirty years later, this astrological energy returns. How will it manifest itself in today's world? First of all, you had a practice run 30 years ago, but you've also worked with this energy in past lives. Use your energy-sensing skills of today to re-evaluate those other experiences with this energy pattern. Use self-guided visualization to go back to the 60's and/or back to any past life that comes into view, refreshing your memories of how to work with Pisces/Saturn energy effectively. Those times were practice, and today is the primary event for which you prepared. Your group's plans are unfolding at a faster pace, fueled by this compatible astrological energy.

Planetary Energy Fluctuations

Of course, another critical influence comes from Earth's own planetary energy. Energy-sensitive people have already noticed the fluctuations in the energy flow of the planet. The new energy, faster and more intense, has not yet modulated into a stable pattern. Stabilization will occur over the next three to five years, with the planetary energy growing steadily smoother and more dependable. Remember the "energy spikes" we spoke of in the third section of this book? The current planetary experience is the same phenomenon. Metaphorically speaking, the cause for this turbulence in the planet's energy is much like what happens when you add liquid to a half-filled container. As you pour in additional liquid to fill the container, turbulence occurs in the water as the new liquid blends with the existing liquid. No matter how gently you pour, there is a disruption of the balance inside the container. Earth is the container, and planetary energy is the liquid. The pouring in of the new energy was the energy shift itself, and current energy conditions (like energy spikes) are caused by the "sloshing around," as the two energies blend together and balance themselves.

How do these energy fluctuations affect you and your lifeplan? This is a rather tricky time in everyone's plans, because you are working to move forward while the ground beneath your feet is moving, like an earthquake is underway! Obviously, you need to go forward gently and a little bit slower than you might wish. It is critical to use *harmonic blending* in all things–new blending with old, risk blending with stability, dreams blending with reality, new skills blending with old habits, new desires blending with old expectations. At times, you may feel you are just creeping along on your hands and knees. *That is okay!* As long as you sense forward movement, perhaps slow but moving steadily, you are doing great!

The energy fluctuations are very strong right now, but they will gently decrease in frequency and intensity over time. In several months, you can walk slowly instead of crawling along on your hands and knees. In a several more months, you can begin to walk faster and faster. As the energy becomes more modulated over time, you will be able to run along at top speed once again. Remember that the base energy of the planet has shifted. You may be just "crawling"–but on a moving sidewalk like those found at airports; you are covering a lot more distance than you realize. Even if you stand still, holding a handrail for support, you are still moving forward! It is fine to go slowly now. If there's a period of stability where you can safely move faster, you will be guided into stronger activity for awhile, meaning more changes, more lessons, and an increased sense of movement in your life. Be gentle with yourself.

You may already feel intense anticipation, for almost all of you are moving into active preparation for your primary life work. If there was ever a time in your life when you wanted to run fast, this is it! However, current planetary energies make it very hard to hold your balance for long periods of time. If you try to run over a moving surface, there is much more risk of falling flat on your face. Then, you may blame yourself for falling down! Awareness of the external circumstances is important, as it helps you understand that you are not at fault for moving slowly or for falling down.

Just creep along, remembering that your own effort is magnified and intensified by the dharmic moving sidewalk that effortlessly carries you forward.

Even as you are jostled about by this turbulent planetary energy, you need to seek out balance in your life. Overall balance is best obtained by a steady, continual shifting of attention: from day to day matters, to your goal out in the distance in front of you. If you focus too long on one or the other, you increase the risk of getting tripped by obstacles or rough spots in your pathway, or getting off target with your long-term goal. Keep this in mind, particularly during the next couple of years.

Use every skill available to stay neutral or positive. Everything you've learned through past personal growth work and life experience is in your "toolbox" of techniques; use these tools to stay balanced at this time. Do not get upset if you occasionally stumble and fall down, because *as long as your energy is neutral,* you can just sit there and will continue to move slowly forward. Rest up a bit before starting to crawl again, and take another look at your long-term goal for motivation. At this point, you are more like the tortoise than the hare, especially if you want gentle harmonic movement. We cannot repeat this enough: *It only feels slow. You are actually moving along quite rapidly.* You want to concentrate on safe little baby steps; running a short high-speed sprint is not the feeling you want. When a situation begins to feel unstable, back off and allow the passage of time to stabilize things.

With regard to lifeplans, most of you are entering the final preparation phase, which often includes "final exams" to see if you are complete with old issues or lessons from the past. If you flunk one of these exams, you will find yourself in an intensive review of that lesson. Don't berate yourself. Just concentrate on completing your review work. Imagine that you are a performer, like a dancer or singer, who is about to give the performance of a lifetime. You carefully warm up, then practice the trickiest part of your song or dance a few times for confidence. This is why these final exams and reviews often concern the most difficult of all your issues.

Today's work makes things go smoother in the next phase. Do not worry that all this practice means you are not ready.

If you are in Wave One, and so, first in line among the interconnected lifeplans, you are just now getting warmed up to the new energy. Remember that Wave One people are energy workers who plan to invent new energy methods and techniques. Obviously, the wild fluctuations in the planetary energy affect your work at this time. For this reason, all the waves are really just warming up in a sense. Many in Wave One are at work now, but results are fluctuating just like the planetary energy, at least for a while. People in Waves Two and Three must wait for the creations of the Wave One workers, so everything is being made ready *very early*, with plenty of time to spare. We tell you this as another reinforcement for letting things move along at the seemingly slow pace of today.

The best activities for you at this time are things that help you modulate your personal energy flow. In general, this includes: light physical exercise, gentle energy techniques, flow activities of any sort, meditation, singing, dancing, drawing, painting, cooking, gardening, or whatever makes you feel whole and balanced. You might think you are wasting your time, but it is *extremely important* that your personal energy system is strong and open for the next stage in your work. Time spent at such activities is time well spent.

If you have spells of negative energy, work to achieve neutral as soon as possible. Realize that the negative influences in your environment are getting stronger. Those around you who have not chosen growth with joy are beginning to achieve their goal of growth with pain-which means there is plenty of negative, painful energy around to pump into your own system. We are aware of the pain you might feel when someone close to you is choosing the painful pathway-choosing illness, depression, anger, or even death. We are aware that reaching neutral energy about illness or death of a loved one can be very difficult. When you feel helpless, unable to shift out of negative, turn for assistance to another soul who is clearly choosing joy. You can one day return the service to that person (or another). This kind of teamwork is helpful when both parties (the hurting one and the helper) understand how to manage the interaction; how to help the one with negative energy without dragging down the other, more positive person.

Your goal in all things is deliberate, conscious action–whether manifesting, using flow energy, helping others, or whatever you are doing. Every minute of every day, be awake! Live deliberately!

Chapter Sixteen

Clear Your Pathway

Part A – Where Do You Start?

Any good navigator knows you must start your calculations by looking around at the present surroundings. In order to plot your pathway into a joyful future, you need to determine your current position. There are several kinds of markers and guideposts you may use as you examine where you are in this lifetime—some obvious, and some that are hidden from casual view. You may find it helpful to write down your evaluation of your present status.

A Review of Your Current Position

- ✧ Review the status of your relationships—all varieties. Look for what pleases you about them as well as what needs improvement. Remember that areas of conflict are where your highest growth potential lies.

- ✧ Review how you spend your time each day, rating the segments by how negative to positive you feel during *and after* each activity. You can use any sort of rating system, such as numbers (-10 to +10) or maybe colors (assign a hue to each mood). Your goal is to increase the positive time, and decrease or eliminate all negative time. *Tip:* Watching television is a neutral activity for most people. For more joy, experiment with ways to increase time spent in *FLOW* activities.

✧ Mentally review what effect you have on people with whom you have daily contact: close family members, friends, people at work, acquaintances, even store clerks and bus drivers. All day to day interactions are merely opportunities for souls to make contact. As you move through each day, you leave an energy trail behind you, like the wake that extends behind a boat cruising through water. Metaphorically speaking, what does your wake look like? Is it rough and choppy, overturning small boats without your knowledge? Is it so small it can hardly be seen? Are there smiling dolphins playing in your wake, drawn by your energy? Please be aware that only sincere and heart-felt interactions make true soul contact.

✧ How much do you laugh and smile each day? Again, sincere and heart-felt feelings of joy are the most meaningful. Belly-laughs add years to your life! Try hard to add laugh lines to the wrinkles on your face.

✧ Examine how well you and your physical form work as a team. Are you comfortable in your body? Whenever you and your body are "out of synch," it feels like wearing shoes that are either much too small or way too large. Just as pinched toes or blistered heels signal ill-fitting shoes, your body tries to let you know what it needs for good health (like food, sleep, sex, or protection from perceived danger). Good teamwork with your body leads to a more comfortable fit. If you think of your physical form as "soul clothing," how well would you say yours fits right now? How does the style and color. fit with your image of yourself? Is there anything you need to change?

✧ Meditate on how you drive down the road of life. Ask your guides to show you a little internal movie of this, using guided meditation. What is your speed? Your driving skill level? Your driving style? Compare this metaphor to how you actually drive an automobile. There is tremendous validity in comparing the two. Are you holding up traffic by driving slowly in the fast lane? Are you weaving in and out between the other cars, occasionally causing a crash, leaving wreckage behind you? Are you so tentative you always get someone else to drive you around? Experiment with changes in your style behind the wheel, both internally and externally. You see, they are actually the same thing!

✧ Use your dreams to allow your guide's input. For two weeks, record all dreams. During Week One, ask for dreams that define your current position. During Week Two, ask for dreams that show the pathway ahead. Remember, the guides will provide this information in metaphor. Many times, it is easier for a trusted friend or companion to help you work through the interpretation of your dreams. The "realness" of the dream experience seems to cloud the ability of the dreamer to discover the meaning of the metaphors. Get a dream partner with whom to trade dream-talk.

✧ Examine your lifetime from the roots (back in childhood) to the sprouting of the buds (here and now). The actual time for full bloom is getting closer and closer! The full life cycle of this metaphorical plant is your current lifetime, viewed in its entirety. We suggest this examination to help you understand more about yourself and your current state, while also taking you forward to later plans. Allow your guides to provide a visual image of your "growth" in this manner, whether you see yourself as a large oak tree or an exotic African violet. Next, use your skills to visualize any improvements to your "plant-self" that you need to consider, showing your wishes and intentions to the Universe in this manner. Whatever is needed in your life to help you turn these improvements into a physical reality will turn up as harmonically as possible.

Put Your Goals into Tangible Form

There are many ways to send out your intentions to the Universe. Tangible expression of your intentions helps to clarify and remind you of *your own* dreams and plans. Visible goals also intensify the amount of energy directed toward an intention. Use one method or several, whatever feels comfortable.

✧ Express your goals, describe your desires, own your dreams! Write down your goals in an "Intention Book," or simply jot them down on scratch paper. Most importantly, use completely positive wording. Say what you *do* want, ignoring whatever you do not want.

✧ Show your goals in a visual or auditory way, rendered in either realistic or abstract form. Create a painting. Make a collage. Write your own song, or choose any song you like as a meaningful anthem.

✧ Decide on a symbolic representation for any goal: the sun, the moon, a rose, a lion, or whatever else you find meaningful. Like Native American totems, the symbol you choose can represent some trait or ability you wish to gain. Surround yourself with meaningful objects that hold a variety of symbols for your goals. You need not go out and buy these things. You can use something you already own simply by establishing a symbolic meaning for the item. Match up your favorite objects to your wishes and intentions. There is great fun in this exercise.

✧ Store your goals in a crystal, placing them there with your thought energy. A good crystal, well-endowed with your own energy pattern, amplifies the output of your goal-focused energy. The crystal need not be large, nor expensive or perfectly unflawed. The attunement of the crystal to your personal energy is the most important factor. A well-attuned crystal *feels* good in your hand.

✧ Share your goals with other people, for this expands the energy, propelling the goals forward. Energy Circles, as mentioned in Section Three of this book, are useful to consciously and deliberately energize the intentions of a small, comfortable group.

Personal Lifeplans

Please recall that each lightworker created an individual lifeplan, complete with alternative and contingency plans in case of last minute predicaments. Your White House group has been in a final preparation phase in recent months and years. In a sense, that stage is officially over for all of you. When the planetary energy hit 90 mph, the "pre-game warm-up" began; recent astrological changes mark the game kick-off, officially starting the event! Everyone enters active lifeplan work within the next five years. The line between preparation and the "real thing" is very nebulous. Readiness often requires shifting into a new position, moving yourself closer to primary lifeplan activities. *Even if you are still preparing, that preparation is part of your cosmic work!* After kick-off, every player—even those on the bench—must be ready to take over a key position on the playing field.

Your intense anticipation will subside as action starts, but your anxiety levels on particular decisions and choices may intensify. Your intuitive self knows that some seemingly small choices are quite powerful. Sometimes a little nudge at the right time creates an efficient flow—meeting up with certain people, hearing about a special book, reading a particular item in the newspaper, etc. Use your best skills to stay focused and joyful, especially when you sense that a critical turning point is occurring. Laughter and humor are extremely helpful to maintain your balance.

In one sense, there is little content difference between the final dress rehearsal and the first performance, but there is a great difference in the energy exchange that happens. Every action, every choice, every thought you have at this time is propelled by powerful, intensified energy. The effect of every person-to-person interaction is magnified. Be conscious. Be aware. Be deliberate. We cannot guide you every moment, but your own intuition can, if you are open to the input. Conscious awareness of the energies around you is the best doorway to understanding what is happening and why it is happening. Don't be asleep at the wheel. Keep all your senses alert, all *six* of them.

You will find your personal situation adjusting and changing more rapidly now. Responsibilities that are not a part of your primary lifeplan will fall aside. Don't fight the tide of any changes that come. If some of your friends or family seem to pull away from you, allow that distance without pain or sadness; space is being made for task companions and lifeplan work. Many individuals who appear (or reappear) at this time are directly involved in your plans. If you cannot discern the immediate connection, be alert to clues and insights. They will also appear.

Be deliberate in your conversations. Speak what comes into your mind, even if it sounds a bit unusual. Listen closely to what people say to you. This is a time when coded signals are used frequently, triggering another phase of the lifeplan activities. You may speak coded phrases to others, and you may hear coded phrases spoken to you. Sometimes, you might sense something dynamic happening during a seemingly commonplace interaction. If so, your intuition and your personal guides are helping you follow some of the work your Higher Self is undertaking outside your conscious awareness. There are many levels of awareness possible on the physical plane; if you wish to be aware of the more delicate and refined energies, you must pay attention! Every time you interact with another person, you have an opportunity to increase your energy awareness.

As you may already realize, we enjoy our work as guides. At our level of existence, it is not possible for us to spend energy in a manner that does not bring us joy. What makes us most joyful?

Whenever we figure out some artful new way to present an old message, something to remind you of the vital basics. You see, the big things do not pull you down as much as the cumulative effect over time of a multitude of small things. For this reason, we will outline a few of the small things that can add up to significant amounts of energy loss.

- *Keep all waste flowing in a timely fashion.* Work to keep waste from piling up. This includes *any form* of waste—physical, emotional, or spiritual. The easiest place to start is your physical environment, such as your home or office. Take a few minutes each day to sift through one little pile of collected "stuff" —on a counter, on your desk, in your briefcase or purse. Each time you toss out (or recycle!) something useless to you, a space is created for something new to enter your life. This need not be a major spring clean-up, just one little area each day. Over time, all the garbage in your life is gently cleared away with minimal effort.

- *Drink plenty of water.* Your energy system is very sensitive to water, while other liquids like soda, coffee, tea or milk, tend to influence one part of the body more than another. One of the easiest ways to boost your energy levels is to flush the system with water. Right now, the new planetary energy creates an increased need for more fluid in your physical body. Of course, toxic water is not good for you, but use your intuition in choosing the best water to use. Many "purified" bottled waters have had all the electrical energies removed in the process of purification. Sometimes, plain tap water has more life to it in this sense. Trust your inner guidance on this.

- *Create space for play in your life.* Is your "play" too structured? Is there any child-like joy and spontaneity left in it? Do you feel okay to just sit around sometimes, floating, without a goal or purpose? How do you feel about exploring a new place or activity? When you "play," do you get extremely competitive? Do you have fun only if you win? Look at what is playful in your life, and evaluate it by the standards of a four year old. If you cannot recall how you felt about play at four years old, go spend some time with children between three and five years old. Join in their activities and relearn to play. It requires some emptiness—some space and time to be filled up with activity. If you know *how* to play, then just create some space and time—and *do it!*

✧ *Add small touches of beauty and grace to your surroundings.* Buy some fresh flowers. Arrange your fruit in a glass bowl so you can see the bright colors. Buy a papaya just to look at. Light some candles for dinner, even if you're eating alone! Toss a colored scarf over a lampshade for a soft glow in your bedroom. What is the point here? You are focusing on the current moment by providing yourself with sensory pleasures that have no potential for negative consequences. Also, any increase in beauty represents an increase in energy, thus, these pleasant touches are like little batteries that recharge the energy of your environment.

✧ *Get plenty of sleep.* The intensification of planetary energy is *very* likely to cause short periods of disrupted sleep. Although your body can sustain this, your "astral work-schedule" might be fractured if you cannot get to sleep. Remember, you often leave your body while sleeping—conducting meetings and preparing for upcoming activities when you are awake. Sometimes you will *need* to sleep, just to get something taken care of on the astral plane. Have some patience with yourself, and don't be concerned that your body is falling apart.

Part B – A New Skill: Reality-Shifting

In this section, we introduce a completely new concept: reality-shifting. From now on, due to the intensified energy on the planet, you can use this method for strong, quick results. Reality-shifting can trigger instantaneous changes in your situation, instigated by your consciousness! We begin with the conceptual underpinnings, followed by precise and specific information on how to put reality-shifting to work in your daily life.

What is Reality Shifting?

This phrase describes a process where you consciously and deliberately move from one reality to an alternative one. Please recall earlier material where we described how the choices you make moment to moment move you through time. Each choice has a polarity, formed by the two aspects of the polarity. One option moves you toward joy/love; it is paired with another option that moves you toward pain/fear.

At each instant of choosing, your position on a pain/joy spectrum is adjusted. On this spectrum, there is a range of pain from intense to slight, shifting into a small neutral zone in the center, then moving into the joy range that also goes from slight to intense. If you are firmly in the joyful zone, a few pain choices just shift you into a lesser degree of joy; if you are in the slightly painful part of the pain zone, your pain choices increase your pain. When you choose to shift reality, you change the entire spectrum to a new range; you change to a new yardstick, rather than just changing your position on the old yardstick. Obviously, most people who reality-shift are choosing to move into a more joyful reality, but it is also possible to shift into a more painful reality. For this reason, we will provide full and complete details for the technique of reality-shifting, and we recommend that you practice on small issues before tackling the bigger ones.

If you have studied time line theory or alternate realities, you may have a pretty good idea of how this shifting process works in theory. For instance, how would things be different today if the U.S. had decided against nuclear bombs to end the war with Japan in the 1940's? How might American history have been affected if

President Lincoln had never been assassinated? According to time line theory, certain events and choices occur at nexus points, which are like forks in the time line. When you put enough energy into a particular option (even if you later decide against that option), an alternate reality splits off from the primary time line. There is another "you" that goes down that pathway, exploring the results of that option. In a sense, everything you ever imagined is really happening in another reality, on another time line. This is the true power of your consciousness.

It is as if a large cinema complex were showing many, many films that depict your life; however, at particular points in each film, the script departs into other scenarios. In Film #14, you might drown in a swimming accident at the age of nine instead of being saved by your cousin. In Film #39, you might marry your high-school sweetheart instead of your current spouse. In Film #117, you might crash your car and break your leg instead of having a close call with no damage. In Film #497, you might have a heart attack instead of a heart*burn* attack. All these movies are actually in progress right now, but you are experiencing only one of them. When you reality-shift, you get up and move to another theater. You can understand why it is vital to deliberately choose what you want, moving into a reality that is more joyful.

At times, you might have an inkling of what is going on in some of your other realities. Think back to the events and decisions that would have lead you off into a very different life. The nexus points of your life are often easy to discern *after* the fact, and sometimes very small decisions have large consequences. For instance, if you had decided you were too tired to go to a party one Saturday night, you might have missed meeting your current spouse. It is very important that you develop an awareness of when major nexus points are occurring in your life; the most common way souls get off track from their lifeplan is by being "asleep" when they hit a critical fork in the road. Sensitivity toward these nexus points is also necessary to deliberately and successfully shift realities.

How to Reality-Shift

There are three segments of a reality-shifting event: sensing a nexus, choosing a positive alternate reality, and moving through the doorway. Each segment may pass in a few seconds or minutes, or perhaps even days, but you seldom have more than a week or two (at most) before the alternate reality moves too far away to recapture in a single nexus event, i.e. one choice. Please understand that you have countless opportunities to choose each day, but not every choice is a nexus (a critical decision that manifests a major time line variation).

1. *Sensing the nexus.* You must use your intuitive abilities, for many nexus points are not logical or predictable. However, sometimes you *can* and *do* use logic to discern a critical decision such as which job to take, which house to buy, or which person to marry. Most people are very aware of the importance of nexus points such as these, and generally deliberate carefully before making a decision. Oddly enough, however, reality-shifting is generally more successful when using the more subtle nexus points. There is tremendous impact from these "hidden" nexus events; your life is commonly redirected and reshaped through occurrences that seem very minor as they happen. Only in retrospect is the true impact observable.

   Nexus events are often surrounded by a slightly different energy. Seek to understand and recognize the subtle difference. The easiest feeling to isolate is often a mild tension and/or anticipation regarding a mundane choice or event. Your conscious mind is not fully aware, and your subconscious triggers this delicate sensation. Begin by studying your life up to this point in time, isolating two or three nexus points that were not obvious to you when they occurred, but which you now know impacted your life significantly. Next, ask your guides to provide stronger signals to catch your attention when another nexus occurs in your life.

2. *Choosing a positive alternate reality.* The most helpful skill for this aspect of reality-shifting is good visualization ability. By this, we mean that you can use your inner eye to collect information. All of you use this skill frequently, but out of habit rather than with deliberate intent. This is a key difference! Your Higher Self and your guides provide clear options and information to you if you can just pay more conscious attention! In order to be increasingly focused, we advise that you establish a "mini-ritual" for yourself, a formal sequence that brings more control to your thought process as you explore the consequences within various alternate realities. You can use your mind to shift from one to another, checking them out before selecting one as your preference—like going there for a short visit without your body.

Your mini-ritual helps you quiet the noise (both internal and external) that blocks your ability to clearly perceive the different options. Of course, you may set up your reality-checking ritual in any form that works for you. There is not a single or "right" way to do this. However, we describe a potential system here, one that uses the guided visualization method provided in Section Two, Chapter Eight of this book.

Take a few minutes of uninterrupted, quiet time. Be sure you are firmly in a neutral or positive state. Spend a few minutes building your energy flow with breathing techniques. Then, light a large candle to represent the bright intensity of your inner flow of energy. (Strengthening your personal energy makes it easier for your Higher Self to input information/energy to you.) Imagine that you are a film director who is screening a recently edited version of your latest movie (your own life). You have filmed many versions of this movie, but you are deciding which version you prefer. At the current nexus point, the movie stops and the projectionist asks you which version to play next. You can see as many versions as you want, stopping and starting them as you like, comparing them to one another.

Put your consciousness in a receiving state, similar to how you feel when watching movies or television. This attitude usually helps the information come to you with more clarity. Sometimes it helps to "rewind" the action. Go back to events that have already happened, then let the variation of events at the nexus point flow smoothly towards its outcome. Your goal is to see where each alternate takes you over time, and how positive that outcome is over the long-term. If you are at a minor nexus, there are only small variations from one reality to another; if you are at a major nexus, the alternate realities diverge more distinctly. Go ahead and let the movie run a little while, since some outcomes require the longer perspective to become fully evident.

3. *Moving through the doorway.* Once you have selected the alternate reality you prefer, how do you shift into it? Remember, whatever you think about is energized with your thoughts and emotions; made more likely to happen. Therefore, each option you consider has at least some degree of energy infused into it. However, the most energized realities are the ones that trigger strong emotions, for this intensifies the energy. If you came across a reality with an outcome that triggered a strong negative reaction (such as fear or pain), you must place *more* emotion into the desired positive reality. You ultimately place yourself in the reality with the strongest energy attachment, whether negative or positive.

For many of you, fear of what you do not want is stronger than desire for what you *do* want, and this is a very big problem. The solution? Awareness that leads to change. Deliberate use of the strongest creative force in the Universe— your consciousness. If you come across a reality that is negative for you, cut off the energy to it. This is sometimes accomplished simply by not thinking about it. When dealing with strong issues, however, particularly repressed issues that are fighting to get out, ignoring them may be impossible. The fear energy is stored inside your body, magnetizing you toward choices that match the fears inside you, bringing them to you again and again in hopes you will learn the lessons. This causes people to get in the same situation over and over, even when they resist. You must find a way to dump the fear or pain energy-magnets inside your system using techniques which remove energy blockages. Stop the vicious cycle which blocks your movement into a more positive reality.

You are the author of a novel, writing your life as you live it. Sometimes, you write yourself into a corner—into a situation that does not seem to have a positive way out. Much like writers for soap operas on television who must sometimes stretch believability in order to bring back a character that was killed in a previous episode, you can do the same. This is how miracles manifest—reality-shifting that stretches believability. Sometimes, you will sense the mechanism that brings about the shift; most of the time, however, the maneuvers are far too complicated for you to predict. For that reason, concentrate your energy on the version of reality that feels best and most positive, even if it seems a little vague here and there. With practice, you may learn to discern a "click" of sorts when you successfully complete a jump into an alternate reality.

One of the strangest aspects of reality-shifting is that only your intuition can tell you when you have been successful. If you manage to jump into a more positive reality, it will seem like the *only* one to you (as you live it). For this reason, the most important first step into reality-shifting is the general awareness that other options exist. Being inside the time-space/continuum makes it very difficult for you to observe the full array of realities. This limitation is required so you can concentrate on your issues and lessons, but you requested that we awaken you to these other realities.

Reality-shifting is a critical part of your work here on Earth. Operating as a team, your White House group seeks to shift the reality of the whole planet! This occurs when individual souls on the planet make their personal choices of reality. As your group chooses love over fear, again and again and again, the "average energy" of the planet is adjusted. At any given moment, your consciousness shifts to the version of Earth that best matches your own energy. Look around you; the world that you live in is a direct mirror of your internal consciousness. Everything around you represents a part of yourself.

As a species, humans on Earth have many possible realities at this time. Every day, however, the range of choices has been getting fractionally more positive. In other words, the worst possible option today is not as negative as the worst possible option last week, and the best possible option has gotten more positive. If you are looking at the middle section of the spectrum, there is little discernible difference, but over time, these incremental movements create a vast change. In the last 20 years, you have gone from an average 15 percent probability that a nuclear bomb would be used, to an improved, current reality with less than 1 percent probability. You can use your skills to sense alternate realities. If you want to explore planetary choices, use the film director method to check out the current range of options available to the planet on any given subject. Be sure to energize the most positive one!

From Carol: I have a personal story here to add to this topic. Each bit of information I channel provides a tremendous amount of insight to me personally. Michael often works with me through the events and experiences of my life to help me understand the topics more deeply, so I'm not just typing the words. I imagine the same sort of thing happens to some of you readers, too. Many times, I feel led to read a certain book or to see a particular movie. Such sources of input start me thinking about a particular topic which ends up as the main subject of channeled information. In this way, I get warmed up to the topics, and it seems to flow more easily when I actually sit down to type.

Just before channeling the previous information, I had an experience involving this reality-shifting topic. I had recently finished reading *The Fifth Sacred Thing*, a wonderful novel by Starhawk that includes many metaphysical concepts put into practice as part of the action in the story. One of the main characters is a trained healer who had been taught to beware of creating "the Bad Reality" for herself. The concept of alternate realities was not new to me, but to consciously shift realities in the midst of high activity (as in this story) was new and very interesting to me. As I finished the book, I developed a problem with my left jaw—a dull, aching pain, with no obvious source. It was fairly easy to ignore, but irritating. Finally, I went to the dentist. The Dental Assistant who took the X-rays was perplexed. She said that it might require a root canal. "Yuk!" I thought. While the X-rays were being developed, I sat alone in the dental chair.

I decided the root canal was a Bad Reality and I wanted the Good Reality instead. I imagined the dentist saying to me, "It's just this simple little problem here. Very easy to fix." I could not figure out exactly what it could be, but I created an opening in my belief system that *something* beside that root canal existed as a more pleasant option. Something clicked inside me. The dentist came in and informed me that part of one tooth was causing my bite to be slightly off on the left side. I was grinding my teeth at night, causing muscle pain from the bite problem. He painlessly ground off a fractional amount of that tooth in about two minutes. I made it to the *Good Reality* that easily! I felt like someone who had painted themselves into a corner, but then painted a doorway marked "Exit" which really opened!

Chapter Seventeen

You've Already
Crossed the Border

The border . . . the line between the old, languid energy and the new, intensified energy. You danced right across that border, most of you completely unaware of the significance. Think about the borderlines between countries. The lines are well-defined on a map, but in the physical experience, you need special road signs or border guards to let you know when you have crossed from one country to another. In a similar fashion, we are your border guards, and we declare that your planet has already officially entered the new energy zone!

How is this zone different? What do you need to do now? Your first goal as a lightworker is to maintain your own focus completely on joy. *Immediately* take action to shift to neutral as soon as you observe any negative, fearful energy in your own system. When you are not feeling neutral to positive energy, you have nothing to offer other souls at this critical time. Do whatever it takes to get yourself into the habit of neutral/positive and out of all negative energy habits. Your entire system will help you. If a certain activity is likely to trigger a negative energy from you, your body may give you a strong signal to stay home (a headache, etc.) Your intuition can be tuned to operate in high gear—volume turned to the maximum—just to be sure you get clear, distinct signals. Please pay attention!

It is also a time to smile at others, reach out a friendly hand, make someone else's day more joyful through small actions. You may have heard of the recent trend for guerrilla kindness directed at strangers, also called "random acts of kindness." This popular trend was created and promoted by a particular group of lightworkers, souls working in conjunction with your group. Start practicing right away. Get into the habit during the upcoming days, for you want to develop a routine of such behaviors. The response you get to these actions intensifies your own joyfulness, as well. Another part of the plan.

Now, a return to our information on nexus points and reality-shifting. Through the upcoming ten years, there will be several opportunities for planetary reality-shifting, nexus points where the planet as a whole chooses between joy and pain. The first planetary nexus point occurred in April 1994, and it was a success. That nexus was the first of several critical choices for the planet, the outcomes of which are shaped by the energies of all current occupants of the planet. In a sense, the nexus of April '94 was the point when you crossed the border.

Such nexus points determine major planetary consequences, and this first one closely matched your group's prediction (and intention) of growth with joy rather than growth with pain. The overall planetary energy chosen at this nexus point will be in effect for approximately two years, with a few additional, minor nexus points along the way. In mid-1995, another "election" or nexus, will occur, followed by three more unevenly spaced over the subsequent eight years. This creates a possibility of five quick "jumps" into more and more positive realities in the upcoming decade. We refer to them as elections because, in a sense, all humans on the planet consciously or unconsciously cast a vote for joy or pain.

Earth last had planetary nexus points of this intensity long before any recorded human history, and the planet has *never* had such a quick succession of so many major pathway shifts in such a short period of time. It is the magical time you have planned and waited for. It is the time to use all that you have learned and practiced—preparing for so many months, years, and lifetimes. Each nexus involves critical mass, so be sure to develop a habit of constantly choosing joy. The dates of the other elections are not significant, as you need to be perpetually in joy or neutral at all times. If you need to know the dates for any reason, your guides will let you know. It is time to turn inward for your information.

We will add that the political and economic systems on the planet will most likely react strongly to these new energies. Expect amazing and even shocking events to continue to unfold over the next several years. Be assured that each of these events leads the planet into wholeness, harmony, and balance. Pathways to wholeness may require some dismantling of systems which block progress. Some conclusions are required to make way for some beginnings. Prepare yourself for this. Understand it as you observe it happening.

You likely feel a huge expansion in your capacity for joy during this time—even at this moment! Is your heart beginning to thump harder at our words? Is some deep inner part of your being thrilled at this confirmation of your anticipation? Let these sensations move through your system. Allow yourself to completely and fully *feel the joy of this moment!* You have planned and worked for many, many lifetimes to be here at this time.

More about the April 1994 Planetary Nexus

We feel sure that each of you already sense that one of the joyful realities is where you now find yourselves. However, the nexus in April 1994 was not a simple choice between two realities— one joyful and one painful. Remember, there are countless different reality paths. For the purpose of simplification, observers of alternate realities tend to group similar realities into clumps. Of course, this grouping can vary greatly depending on the criteria used to categorize the different possible realities.

In order to explain the results clearly, we must first explain our method of grouping alternate realities. We judged innumerable realities and rated them according to their levels of pain energy versus joy energy. From our perspective (outside the time/space continuum) and with use of something you would consider a "cosmic computer," we developed a graduated scale of possible realities. At the original inception of this scale, the range of outcomes went from -10 (the most painful) up through 0, and on up to +10 (the most joyful). The first version of this scale was done by you lightworkers some 300-500 lifetimes ago, at the beginning of your adventure on planet Earth. Remember, current "membership" of your family of lightworkers is rising! You gather new members every day as part of your plan is to embrace any soul who wants to bring in light to this planet.

On the scale of possible realities, the most painful possibility (-10) was annihilation of all sentient life on the planet. This probability hovered at a low 2 percent probability for most of your incarnations on this planet, although it jumped to an increased probability of about 20 percent during one or two short-term crisis periods in the last 40 years. This was mostly due to the invention of nuclear technology. From the beginning of your work here on Earth, your group has known that there would be a critical time frame in the final 50 years or so before the actual transformation began, and so it was. Ancient and recent predictions of catastrophes and cataclysms were all reminders to be wakeful during the critical time. In the past five to ten years, enough light energy was activated to shift the range of possible realities, dropping off the ones below -5. Knowledge can change outcome, which is the key to how these intensely negative outcomes were avoided. Light energy brings information, and information triggers knowledge in those who ingest the light. Do you see why you lightworkers are here?

Please recall that a planetary nexus point is a major conjunction in the time/space pathway you are travelling. There are countless small adjustments made each day, similar to lane changes on a major freeway, but a planetary nexus point is like that freeway splitting into two different roads with two very different destinations! As you moved into the April 1994 nexus point, the reality scale had already been adjusted upward, with the range now going from -5 through 0 to +10, with the *strongest probability* at about +2 to +3. This was the *expected* position just before this nexus, according to your group's best, original cosmic predictions and plans.

Your plans to reality-jump at this planetary nexus point worked! The "election" results catapulted the entire planet up to a +5 level of joyful outcome. You may be wondering how much to celebrate this outcome, particularly since this was not an unqualified victory of jumping all the way up to +10 in one of Superman's "single bounds!" Remember that faster growth is usually more painful, so your group must gently balance the changes, allowing all occupants of the planet to adjust. (Yes, even joy requires some adjustment!) Of course, +10 is your goal over the long-term, with other planetary nexus points upcoming in the future to use like stair-steps. Our congratulations to you and your entire team of lightworkers!

This is Both a Culmination and a Beginning

This news may trigger intense feelings of excitement and anticipation, a readiness to greet new adventures and new horizons, sensations much like you had at your high school graduation. There may also be a little tinge of fear down beneath these thrills—concerns about your abilities, a little sadness about those who move into other pathways, some confusion about what to do next. These are all the shadow side of the polarity in this situation. In fact, one indication that you are firmly in the appropriate place for these changes, is if you have some feeling of being that young graduate about to tackle the world.

Are you out there at the edge, which is the place where personal growth and transformation occur? The edge is the place between the old and the new, the place where choice occurs, and the place where change happens! If you have any particular part of your life that is "on the edge," this is where to concentrate your effort at this time. Explore the edges of your life—the places where you are not operating on auto-pilot, the activities that require your full awareness and concentration, the situations where you feel magnetized toward something, even if a *tiny* bit frightened of it also! These are the things that get you to stretch yourself, allowing you to feel a burst of improved self-love and self-esteem when you meet the challenge.

Say a loving goodbye to the old baggage of your life. You no longer need those old fears or pains. Allow those who choose other pathways to move forward into whatever their choice-path holds. At the same time, pay attention to those who are coming into view along your current pathway, old friends with arms raised to greet you! Look forward, think forward, act forward.

Joyfully Complete the Transition

There is both a culmination and a new beginning at this time. It is an ending of one phase, signalling the birth of another. For this reason, we present a sequence of ten points to help each of you joyfully complete this transition into the next phase:

✧ Point 1. *Seek to understand the overall plan.* Recognize yourself as a lightworker. You are part of a massive team undertaking which has taken thousands of years to culminate NOW. Expand your focus. Widen your perspective. Allow yourself to remember the core plan, for it is there in your soul's memory.

As you open yourself to these memories of the overall plan, you tend to bring in more of your Higher Self, the part of yourself that holds all your skills and experiences from past lives. It provides access to whatever is needed to complete your lifeplan, even if the plans shift or change! You have not spent a few years or just this lifetime preparing for this time—you have spent hundreds of incarnations developing a wide variety of skills, just so you would be ready for possible last minute changes.

> *Key:* As you seek to understand the overall plan, you will find the forgotten parts of yourself.

✧ Point 2. *Focus on the desired outcome.* Get reconnected to the actual plan itself, which is to bring into common usage energy techniques that have never before been used on this planet. This would have been possible without the present planetary energy transition, but you are using the energy shift for momentum as you push further out at just the right moment! Think of pushing a child on a swing—gentle effort, well-timed action, fun for everybody involved.

Remember, there is only one primary judgement of better/worse within the higher planes of the Universe, and that is efficiency. *Better* is when less energy is used to achieve the desired outcome. Efficiency leads to dharma, the positive effect sustained when less energy is used to achieve an outcome or complete a lesson.

> *Key:* Your group's entire plan is an exercise in creating dharma.

✧ Point 3. *Pay Attention!* There is a response to knowledge, a shift of energy that occurs when awareness enters your consciousness. At the core of quantum physics, your scientists have discovered that quantum particles *behave differently* when they are observed. In other words, the act of noticing creates a change in the outcome. When you pay attention, outcome shifts. This is evidence of the power of your consciousness.

Be aware that you are working on this plan. Be fully awake. Observing the plan as it comes about is important, since it increases your joy to see the results of what you are doing.

Pay attention, for it is necessary to be in the NOW to see what you have accomplished. There is a feedback loop built into the overall plan. Become more aware of this loop and how it works for you personally.

> *Key:* Things happen differently when you pay attention.

✤ Point 4. *Seek out other lightworkers.* This is an important part of how the plan is organized, since there are many team efforts planned. Other lightworkers are part of the feedback loop, responding to your actions and efforts. You progress more efficiently with assistance from other lightworkers.

Figure out how to recognize other lightworkers. Learn how to interpret signals or codes that help you identify one another. For instance, one popular book, *The Celestine Prophecy* by James Redfield, is awakening lightworkers and serving as a signal to help with recognition. Lightworkers are finding one another in *Celestine Prophecy* study groups, computer network discussions, even on airplanes and in offices. Information inside the book is helping people to use spontaneous eye contact and synchronistic occurrences to recognize one another.

> *Key:* Be alert to awakening and connecting of lightworkers.

✤ Point 5. *Seek out the position you have agreed to maintain.* This is a time of transition and shifting, much like the chaotic time before a parade when masses of participants wander around looking for their place in line. Mass confusion does not always mean there is not a plan; it is simply a natural phase within your plan. Do not be alarmed by this sense of chaos.

Because many people are shifting into a different pattern, you will have numerous opportunities to practice letting go of those who are still seeking their pathway. Use your skills at releasing, and concentrate on finding your own spot. It is a very common error during this phase to get caught up in trying to help others find their paths, losing your own way in the process! Develop an awareness of whether you have any information or help for someone else or not. If you cannot seem to get insight quickly, go ahead and release them. The best "error" is on the side of letting go too soon, for they will turn up again if that's what you've done! If you hold them too long (trying to help, of course), you are preventing them from moving on to someone who *does* have the information they need.

> *Key:* People are scurrying all about you;
> do not get caught up in the confusion of
> others as you seek out your own position.

✦ Point 6. *Create a family of lightworkers.* Regardless of your relationships within your genetic family members (which may be harmonious, uncomfortable or indifferent), you will find sustenance and support from your lightworker family. Other lightworkers are able to strengthen your energy levels, which is vitally important to the plan. Many times, the support from your lightworker family members comes from just being together, not necessarily from special effort or work of any kind. Sharing space is sufficient, although adding a little food, talk and laughter is great!

If someone in your current family of relatives and friends keeps putting distance between himself/herself and you, then a space may be opening for a member of your lightworker family to fill. If you have always felt detached, maybe even distant from your birth family, please be aware that you may not have heavy past-life experiences with them like you do with your fellow lightworkers. Earth is a crowded place these days, and you may have used your birth family as a "ticket in the door" (so to speak), allowing you to get here and connect at this time with your family of lightworkers. By the way, we are not saying to dismiss or ignore your "regular" family—unless that is the direction it was already headed before now. No matter the state of your birth family relations, be aware that you have a lightworker family as well.

> *Key:* The lights burn more brightly when lightworkers gather together.

✧ Point 7. *Ask Yourself: What is my secret dream?* That is your seed of light. When you were a child, what did you see yourself doing? More importantly, what did it feel like? This provides you with a semblance of the full power of your soul energy. Your secret dream is probably something big enough that you seldom talk about it. You may have even ignored it for years! Focus on the emotional response, for the power of the lightseed lies within the emotional spectrum of energy. Your logical mind may not think the dream possible, but the emotional response will be clear. Your lightseed is ready to sprout at this time, creating an opening for more personal energy.

Note that the lightseed is a *feeling*—not an occupation or something logical. It is clearly *not* thought-based; it is emotion-based. That is the power of the lightseed. Find the location of the lightseed in your physical form, remembering that it may be a completely new sensation. The lightseeds were not usable until after the April 1994 nexus point.

> *Key:* Meditating on your secret dream is likely to trigger strange and wonderful emotions.

✧ Point 8. *Check your choices against the lightseed.* As you move deeper into the overall group plan, more and more complexity arises. The lightseed provides an internal matrix to help you with the next layer of the plan. Up to this time, you maneuvered from a large map showing the cross-country route from state to state. What happens when you approach the metropolitan area that is your final destination? You must transition to a different map, one with more detail. Using it often requires more attention and concentration. There is a tricky time when you are shifting from the macro-map to the micro-map, a time when both maps may be needed. This is that time.

Develop a personal code to represent the lightseed—an image, the word, a city map even! After using your normal method of making a decision or choice (which gives the view from the larger map), run the decision through the lightseed (which gives the view from the more detailed city map). This double process need not last very long, for it is only a transitional state. After a short while, a year or so, you can shift to the lightseed guidance completely. Be aware that you might get different answers to the two "maps" —and the lightseed is your best guide in that instance.

When you check each choice against the lightseed, you are asking, "Does this take me closer to my secret dream? Is it connected to the overall plan?" There are three possible answers you may receive: closer, further, or "mu." Mu means that the question is inappropriate, or doesn't make sense—like a computer saying, "Does not compute." Checking against the lightseed also provides a method of obtaining the most current, updated information. Please realize that the speeding up of planetary energy increases the speed for changes to your plans! Running a choice through the lightseed is much like making a quick call to the airline right before getting in the car to drive to the airport. A last minute check for current flight arrival time and gate number can save you time and trouble—back to efficiency, again!

> *Key:* Improve your efficiency and flexibility
> by using the updated details that the
> lightseed provides to your decision-making.

✧ Point 9. *Recognize completions and move on.* Learn to identify the signals that tell you when something is concluded. It can be tricky, even difficult, to give up the old and to move into the new. Develop skills at observing this process, learning to conserve energy wasted in extra effort toward something already complete! First of all, *become conscious of body signals.* Almost everyone gets triggered physically when time comes for a change. Next, *question habits constantly!* Habits are a persistent problem only because you do them without thinking. We are not saying to eliminate all habits, but to ask yourself, "Do I want this?" and check it with the lightseed. The only habit to keep for sure is the habit of being tuned in and aware. Stay awake.

> *Key:* When the movie's over, don't just sit
> there in the movie theater—get up and leave!

✧ Point 10. *Respond to what creates a trumpet sound in your heart.* Understand that you now have a strengthened emotional response within your physical system—the lightseed. Your body will literally receive a hefty jolt whenever a doorway to your secret dream opens before you. The lightseed was chosen by you, planted into your physical form, detonated with a timer to activate it at this time. This is the period when you most require clear and unmistakable signals in order to stay on the most joyful and efficient path toward your goal. Be aware of something new inside yourself.

> *Key:* It will be harder to ignore your lightseed
> signals than to follow them!

A Few General Items

Please recall that your group has been planning this for *thousands of years!* Every lightworker is excited and joyful, but that joy increases as individual congruency to the overall plan occurs.

As each person moves into his/her position, those trumpet sounds in the heart will be sounding all around! Your plans are working, and we are pleased to congratulate your successful efforts!

❖ *Seek out experiences that bring about laughter and smiles.* Laughter has a modulating effect on energy—smoothing out the negatives. Any form of laughter is a good thing for your energy system.

❖ *Respond to the requests of others with deliberate awareness.* This is a time of increased polarization, so carefully consider your response to outside requests. Many times, no action or a retreat is in order. This is not a good time to sell joy to an audience that wants pain! You can respond to a request with one of these three potential actions:

1. Comply with the request, setting appropriate limits if needed.
2. Let the energy move around you without touching you (a "mu" response).
3. Remove yourself from proximity.

With any choice, advance carefully. Use light energy. Humor is often helpful, as well as a gentle, calm tone of voice. If you find yourself with a "mu" response, you may actually not hear the request or you might think it was directed at someone else. A "mu" response can mean that you are not involved in the situation, that it has nothing to do with you. A "mu" response can also mean that you are blocking out an issue that needs attention, something that you do not want to deal with. For this reason, you can never assume that an unevaluated "mu" response is always the correct one.

❖ *Focus on the current status of things.* It is only possible to feel joyful when you are in the current moment—not the past, not the future.

✧ *Feel the joy you are creating, for that is your true work at this time!* As a lightworker, your best results do not come from your actions, but from your *feelings!* When you feel joyful, you are pulling in an intense light from the non-physical realms of the Universe, transforming it into a physical plane energy that literally feeds your planet!

✧ *Realize that your truest essence is not your body or even your consciousness, it is your energy.* Your joyful emotions create the magical alchemy that manifests light energy into the physical plane.

Some of this will sound very far-fetched to the skeptical among you. Feel free to have such an opinion. However, look deep inside on an intuitive level, and see how this description feels to your Higher Self. We suspect that you will find some connection point on that level. If you can agree that our version *sounds* good, then you can support this vision with your energy rather than use your energy to build another more realistic, but less joyful future. It is our intention to strengthen the most positive pathway available to you at this time.

Another point to keep in mind here is that we describe the *end product* of the planetary transformation, rather than the *process* taking you from one point to another. As you can imagine, the shift from one paradigm to another is usually messy business. Think of the upheaval generally required to move a family from one house to another—even if the new house is much more spacious and luxurious than the old! The work of transformation is very similar to the work of a household move—opening up hidden storage, sorting and sifting, discarding what is no longer useful, finding new places for old items of furniture (or beliefs), adding new furniture pieces (or belief pieces) to fill up the extra space in a bigger house (or expanded consciousness). What we describe here is the completed home after the move. The tough work of this transformation is what you begin now. Choices and more choices! What to discard, what to keep! These are the activities of the next ten years!

A Look into Earth's Future

In the first section of this book, we described planetwide changes. We spoke of political and economic changes, social changes, changes in education and the arts. At this time, however, we wish to provide an image, a vision of your transformed future. We suggest that you use this to crystallize and intensify your personal intentions for your own future.

Following is a look at the future reality that your group desires to achieve. It is written in the form of a guided meditation. You can use this as a starting point for more exploration of this reality through your own guides. Simply visualize the planet according to what we describe here, particularly at the beginning. Pay close attention to the symbols and shapes, for these are like signposts to lead you to this same reality in subsequent visits.

Imagine that you have gone away in a spaceship for 50 years. You have experienced Einstein's Theory of Relativity by travelling all those years at, or near the speed of light, so you have barely aged in all that time. Take some time to have good sensory connection to the spacecraft, particularly as you re-enter Earth's atmosphere, landing as smoothly as one of today's jet airplanes.

As you leave the ship, you are greeted by a group of four smiling people. At first glance, you notice that everyone's clothing is rather odd-looking. In fact, you notice something unusual about each person. At first, you thought it was brightly-patterned apparel. Now, you realize that each person in the small group gathered around you is wearing soft, comfortable-looking clothing in light, solid colors, but there is a collection of colors seeming to float in the air around each person's body! You realize that these must be auras, but these are not like any auras you have ever seen or read about back before the turn of the century!

The colors are arranged in highly sophisticated designs—some in static arrays that resemble ornate jewelry, while others are actually moving in patterns (sort of like neon signs in Las Vegas!) It becomes clear to you that there is an additional layer of communication happening through these auric energies. What do they mean? You make a mental note to find someone to teach you how to interpret these aura designs. (Note: At any point, like this one in the visualization, feel free to ask for full and complete explanations from people in the vision. Depending on your personal lightseed and lifeplan, you may find a lesson here for you!)

Now your attention shifts from the people to your surroundings. You are in a large, airy chamber with a high ceiling and large windows which look out on a wooded exterior. There is a wonderful variety of indoor plants as well. Your arrival was at the future equivalent of an airport, so the personal atmosphere and decorations are a surprise to you. There are several seating areas, with clusters of people comfortably relaxing and conversing. A group of small children is gathered around a table in one area and appear to be playing some kind of game. Everyone here seems to know one another. There are hand-crafted decorations throughout the spaces—small sculptures on pedestals, a beautifully-carved and painted screen, framed art on the walls. With a shock you notice there are absolutely no advertisements! There is not even a sign visible to identify this location, such as an airline name or gate number. You realize there is pleasant, lively music coming from somewhere. You hear drums, flutes, chants, and some sounds you have never heard before in this context. Is that a whale song?

Next, you are offered a physical examination, with explanations from those greeting you. You are told that medical advances have significantly changed, so this will be a quick and easy process conducted by a short visit with a health consultant.

"Do you mean a doctor?" you ask.

"Not exactly," one greeter replies, smiling. "In the mid-90's,

your physicians were trained with a focus on what a lack of health meant. We have learned that each person controls his or her own physical condition, so the health consultant is a person who can study your aura and help you understand what changes you can make in your own life to increase health. It is a completely different focus, you understand. Don't worry, it will be fun. Health consultants tend to be some of the most lively and amusing people to be around! They often 'prescribe' great remedies like a week at the beach in the sun, or a night out once a week to go dancing! You'll see!"

You walk along with the little group of greeters, into a foyer area—a round room with domed ceiling made of some type of crystal or sparkling substance. There are plants, but no places to sit—the crystalline floor which matches the substance on the dome forms a circular clearing at the center of the room. You realize that there are no windows or visible lighting, but the room is quite light, almost uncomfortably bright.

One of the greeters notices you squinting and explains, "It's an intense form of energy coming from these charged crystals in the floor, walls and dome. This is a pulse point of Earth's energy which has been strengthened to allow for easy teleportation. We use such places as stations to travel easily from place to place. We'll carry you along on our energy, but you'll learn how to do it yourself before long." The next thing you know, you're in another slightly different chamber. It happened in the twinkling of an eye; you felt nothing at all. What will you have to learn to be able to do this yourself?

You and the others enjoy a short outdoor walk after leaving the teleport station. The air tastes sweet, the sky is a vivid blue, and the sun is warm on your shoulders. Obviously, since you've been gone, the problem of pollution has been conquered. You walk past inviting shops and cafes where just about everyone seems to be enjoying pleasant conversation, smiling and talking. You notice out of the corner of your eye that a small child has fallen down and started to cry. The mother, who has a tiny baby in her arms, kneels to comfort the crying child. A grandmotherly woman walking by puts down her shopping bag and offers to hold the infant while the young mother comforts the toddler. Once again, you get the sense that everyone here already knows one another. Make a mental note to ask about that later.

The health consultant turns out to be a young lady of about 20 years of age (or so she appears), who invites you into her home for some tea and a snack. Your greeters agree to return for you later at an appointed time. There has been no explanation to her of who you are, but she seems happy to wait for you to ex-plain yourself whenever you're ready. She busies herself with preparing the tea and a platter of fruit, cheese and crackers. This is not like any trip to the doctor you've ever heard of! You sip tea, munch goodies and ask her some questions about what you've been seeing around you. Occasionally, you get the notion that she is concentrating her gaze just outside some part of your body—then you remember that she's checking out your aura. Well, what about her aura? There's lots of green in the background and splashes of bright colors around the edges. You decide she looks like a flower garden in full spring bloom!

One of your questions is about the woman who stopped to help the young mother in the street. The health consultant ex-plains that a side benefit of visible auras is an improved comfort level when faced with people one doesn't know. "All motivations are revealed in one's aura, so the mother could safely trust her infant to a complete stranger for a few minutes. She could tell that the older woman enjoys babies, and likes a chance to help out a frazzled mom—all that would be easy to see in an aura," she reveals. Then, this smiling stranger adds with a laugh, "You'll soon see how visible auras has changed male/female courting behaviors! Things are simplified now in this area—much easier than what you had to deal with back in the '90's!" You decide to think through all the societal effects of visible auras later when you get some quiet time.

Finished with your tea by now, you and your new friend go out for a look at her garden. Bright, blooming flowers and ripening vegetables surround you.. You notice that everything about you has a careful, undecorated look, so you begin to suspect that the surroundings have actually been created with artful intention—placement of objects in an attractive randomness. Nature's order of things has obviously been honored. This future Earth is a very beautiful place. All the man-made elements—benches, buildings, walkways—seem to have become a part of the natural landscape, but all have subtle artistic touches which personalize them. You see an almost invisible hieroglyph of some unknown meaning on occasional bricks on the buildings. Flat stones at the center of the winding path, but stones with softly rounded tops at the edges. A whimsical folk-art bunny sitting quietly beside a plant you suddenly recognize as carrot. People here must pay attention to the details.

While seated on a garden bench, your health consultant provides her analysis. "First of all, you are in terrific shape for someone of your time . . . not to speak of your age! However, you will want to upgrade your expectations to match what is possible today. You have a couple of little problems that are in the early stages, working at a cellular level only. I can't even say for sure what organ or part of the body would ultimately be affected, because you will not let it get that far, I'm sure."

"At this point, some of your hormonal output is operating in a 'hyper' state—almost as if you were in a constant stage of siege. My studies in health history taught me that this was the most common state for people back in the '90's. Almost all sources of physical stress, such as toxic air and water, have been corrected now, however. You will minimize your emotional stress as you gain comfort with our ways, for we tend to do all things in the most efficient and pleasant manner possible. You have capacity for full joy, as your chakra system is perfectly intact and uninjured, but your energy flow is restricted because you have no goal right now."

"*Your prescription is to find what activities bring you into bliss, and so I recommend that you enroll at U of U, the University of the Universe. Explore all the options for today, seeking out the things that intensify your energy. Meet people with common interests. All the professions are available to you, but most will be almost unrecognizable to your '90's idea of what they involve. Businesses here are owned by the people who operate them—all the people, not just a few. In a sense, everyone is self-employed. Teaching is an extremely popular job these days, mainly because it is such fun, and so rewarding. I spend part of my time teaching, along with this work. In fact, many people choose to become skilled at several jobs, because they enjoy the variety, and because it provides flexibility as community needs change. You can devise a mixture of activities that fits you perfectly, but you must first learn more about what is available. Your pathway will be clear to you as soon as you add it to your list of available options. Just like the two women in the street earlier, there will be people who will sense your needs and help you at the right time. You will join the circle of giving and receiving—giving joy to others by being their student or the object of their assistance, and receiving joy by teaching and helping others.*"

And so your adventure can continue as far as you wish to explore it in your mind—classes at U of U, meetings with other consultants or teachers to answer your questions, a night out on the town, a visit to any city in the world to see how it has changed. Please understand that this is truly a visit to one of your potential futures. The more real it becomes to you, the more energy you have put toward it. Also, please understand that it is *highly* likely that you will truly experience this reality—either in this body or another. Time spent energizing it is a good value.

In Conclusion

Now, our agreement with you is complete; we have reminded you of all the things you asked us to tell you at this time. The only thing left is your individual work! Information is a tool that requires a soul to put it to work, so you and your personal light energy must get busy. We here in non-physical reality can only observe and occasionally provide some words of assistance or inspiration. Action is left up to you who have entered the intensity of the physical form. How easy it is to see the smoothest pathway from here! Yet we remember how difficult it can be from where you are now. It is our highest intention that your wondrous scheme should work, and culminate in consequences that are far beyond what you can even imagine!

We encourage you to move forward with joy, gathering other souls behind you as your marching band and circus parade moves from town to town! Ultimately, your plan succeeds by the creation of such an atmosphere: fun, laughter, excitement, thrills, music, people of all ages drawn together by pure magic! Yes, pure magic is what you seek to create, energized out of an alchemist's mixture of *Love and Light.* We shall all come together at some point to reminisce on this experience. We joyfully await that time.

With love and light to all.

MICHAEL

Recommended Readings

Communication

Straight Talk by Sherod Miller, Ph. D., Daniel Wackman, Ph.D., Elam Nunnally, Ph.D, and Carol Saline. Published by Signet.

Abundance

Wealth Without Risk by Charles Givens. Published by Simon & Schuster.
The Great Boom Ahead by Harry Dent, Jr. Published by Hyperion.

Eastern Leadership

The Tao of Leadership by John Heider. Published by Bantam.

Flow

Flow: The Psychology of Optimal Experience by Mihaly Csikszentmihalyi. Published by Harper & Row.

Leadership and Group Energy Fields

The Leader as Martial Artist by Arnold Mindell, Ph. D. Published by HarperCollins.

Channeling

The Dream Book by Betty Bethards. Published by Inner Light Foundation.
Opening to Channel by Sanaya Roman and Duane Packer. Published by H J Kramer, Inc.

Reality-Shifting

The Fifth Sacred Thing by Starhawk. Published by Bantam.